Praise for
Hesitant to Homeschool?

"*Hesitant to Homeschool?* hits at the heart of what it means and takes to homeschool our children in today's world. It will give any parent considering homeschooling the confidence and the competence to embark on this wonderful journey with knowledge, passion, and joy."

—Alex Kajitani, speaker, author, and California Teacher of the Year

"Curious about homeschooling? Interested in your kids becoming lifelong learners and not just memorizing facts for tests? This book is for you! I wish this book had been around when I first began to consider homeschooling ten years ago! Mandi and Jessica hit all the main questions and alleviate the most common fears parents have about homeschooling. Even as a seasoned homeschooler, I found inspiration and encouragement in these pages and reminders as to why I am equipped to homeschool my children and so are you!"

—Leah Heuss, M.A. clinical psychology, M.A. biblical counseling, mom of four, homeschooler for eight years

"If you ever wanted to gather all the veteran homeschoolers you know in one room so you could ask them a million questions, that is what this book feels like! Not only drawing on their own years of experience, but also those of their many contributors, Mandi and Jessica help first-time homeschoolers navigate the overwhelming world of homeschooling in an organized and encouraging way. Really wish something like this existed when I was starting out!"

—Pauline Chung, mom of six, homeschooler for eight years

"Sometimes when embarking on something brand new, we don't even know all the considerations and questions to ask. Look no further! This well-written book is a thoughtful and thorough, easy-to-read guide that may just give you the boost you need to overcome any fears and replace them with a leap of faith for your child's sake."

—Angela Aymin, cofounder, Off to the Farmhouse

"An outstanding book! It will validate your instincts about homeschooling and demonstrate that you are indeed the homeschooling type. But after you start homeschooling, keep the book handy—it's brimming with fantastic ideas you'll want to explore!"

—Heather Martinson, founder, Celebration Education

"The specialization opportunities and hands-on, passion-based service projects that homeschooling can offer are valuable for preparing students for success in college STEM majors. *Hesitant to Homeschool?* shows how home-taught and team-based activities can develop the self-motivation and desire for discovery that are foundational to learning to conduct research at the collegiate level."

—Steven Dobbs, professor, California State Polytechnic University, Pomona; technical co-advisor for first-place team, California State University Student Research Competition

"As an academic advisor to homeschool families, I wholeheartedly recommend *Hesitant to Homeschool?* for both prospective and seasoned homeschoolers alike. Mandi and Jessica offer clarity and expertise to those considering homeschooling, addressing common concerns with reassuring insight. Each chapter is enriched with real-life experiences and provides practical strategies and encouragement for every stage of the homeschooling journey."

—Heidi Fikse, M.A. Ed., multiple subject teaching credential and education specialist instruction credential

Hesitant to Homeschool?

to

Homeschool?

ANSWERS TO

20

COMMON
QUESTIONS

Jessica Solis Carpinelli
Mandi McArthur

free spirit
PUBLISHING®

Library of Congress Cataloging-in-Publication Data
Names: Solis Carpinelli, Jessica, author. | McArthur, Mandi, author.
Title: Hesitant to homeschool? : answers to 20 common questions / by Jessica Solis Carpinelli
    and Mandi McArthur.
Description: Minneapolis, MN : Free Spirit Publishing, an imprint of Teacher Created
Materials, Inc., 2025. | Includes bibliographical references.
Identifiers: LCCN 2024003415 (print) | LCCN 2024003416 (ebook) | ISBN 9798885546751
    (paperback) | ISBN 9798885546744 (ebook) | ISBN 9798885546782 (epub)
Subjects: LCSH: Home schooling--United States. | Education--Parent participation--
    United States.
Classification: LCC LC40 .S548 2025 (print) | LCC LC40 (ebook) | DDC
    371.04/20973--dc23/eng/20240227
LC record available at https://lccn.loc.gov/2024003415
LC ebook record available at https://lccn.loc.gov/2024003416

Free Spirit Publishing does not have control over or assume responsibility for author or third-party websites and their content. At the time of this book's publication, all facts and figures cited within are the most current available. All telephone numbers, addresses, and website URLs are accurate and active; all publications, organizations, websites, and other resources exist as described in this book; and all have been verified as of May 2024. If you find an error or believe that a resource listed here is not as described, please contact Free Spirit Publishing.

Edited by Cathy Hernandez
Cover and interior design by Michelle Lee Lagerroos

Printed by : 70548
Printed in : China
PO # : 12703

Free Spirit Publishing
An imprint of Teacher Created Materials
9850 51st Avenue North, Suite 100
Minneapolis, MN 55442
(612) 338-2068
help4kids@freespirit.com
freespirit.com

To my loving husband and our wonderful children—your inspiration, support, and love make all things possible.

—Jessica

To Micah, Ruby, and Maisy—you are my sunshine and rainbows. I love homeschooling you. To Marcus, for being my partner and cheerleader in this grand adventure.

—Mandi

Contents

■■ **Introduction** 1

■■ **Part I: I Want to Homeschool, but What If ...** 7

   1. What If I Don't Know the Content? 8

   2. What If I Don't Know How to Teach? 22

   3. What If My Child Won't Learn from Me? 29

   4. What If I Don't Have the Patience? 42

   5. What If I Don't Have the Space? 50

   6. What If I Don't Know What to Do All Day? 57

   7. What If I Can't Afford It? 75

■■ **Part II: Missing Out** 81

   8. Will My Child Miss Out on the School Experience? 82

   9. Will My Child Miss Out on Community? 92

   10. Will My Child Miss Out on Diversity? 101

   11. Will My Child Miss Out on the Academic Classroom? 109

   12. What Will I Miss Out on If I Homeschool? 117

   13. What Will We Miss Out on If We Don't Homeschool? 126

▦ Part III: The Big Ones..135

14. What about Socialization?...136

15. Will My Child Fall Behind?...145

16. What about College? 152

17. Can I Homeschool My Neurodivergent or Gifted Learner?.....................161

18. What about the Naysayers? 174

19. Is It Possible to Work and Homeschool?..............................178

20. I'm Overwhelmed! How Do I Start Homeschooling?..................185

▦ Conclusion 192

Appendices...195

Quick Start Guide 195

Glossary 201

References 205

Index 210

Acknowledgments..213

About the Authors...215

Introduction

> "The best and most beautiful things in the world cannot be seen nor even touched, but just felt in the heart."
>
> —HELEN KELLER (QUOTING HER TEACHER, ANNE SULLIVAN)

Homeschooling is not simply an educational choice, it's a lifestyle that brings beauty and freedom to our lives. We cannot put our finger on one homeschooling element that we do or teach that makes it beautiful; it's all of it. It's the quiet and loud moments during the school day. It's the tears from frustrated math struggles, the regret of wasted time arguing, the shared spark of curiosity, the joy of progress, the heartfelt laughs at silly stories, the memory-making adventures, and the restoring of relationships after a storm—for both parents and children. For us, this beauty floods our homes because we live the whole day together. We have freedom to grapple with and celebrate the little lessons learned in partnership, freedom to make our own decisions with nearly every second of our day. It's amazing for us to get to spend as much time as we want with our children. We get to schedule what we want, when we want, for how busy we want to be. We get to customize the life and learning experiences our family desires.

From our blog, podcast, homeschool conventions, and dozens of Facebook groups, we hear many reasons why people are hesitant to homeschool. They like the idea, but they dismiss it for reasons that aren't always grounded in facts. In this book, we focus on twenty questions that we hear again and again. Whether you think you aren't capable, you believe your children will miss out on opportunities, or there are some big boulders you cannot fathom facing (like working full time), we say: do not let that get in the way of your family's dream life. So, we wrote this book for you: to empower you to make the choice that is right for you and your family.

This is what we want you to know.

Any loving parent *can* homeschool. The next twenty chapters will show you why *you* can. It may take time for you to research and develop your own unique homeschool path, you might need some extra support, or you may need to get creative with navigating schedules. We are here to show you that if you truly want to homeschool, you can do it.

It's true: you are capable of homeschooling. Like many endeavors, homeschooling takes work, perseverance, and—for some—big lifestyle changes (especially for single or working parents). A new responsibility can seem daunting and almost impossible. But we are here to tell you it's possible—and it's beautiful.

You've already done one of the hardest things a person can do: you became a parent. Let's begin by reminiscing about the early parenting years.

Did you parent a newborn? It was a huge lifestyle change! Jobs and careers were put on hold, transportation anywhere took twice as long, and emotional and physical energy were maxed out by lunchtime. Many of us had little or no prior experience changing diapers, nursing a bleary-eyed babe, or bathing a slippery infant. We had no experience functioning after multiple sleepless nights, dealing daily with the colic crying, and we had little patience for the constant drop of the pacifier. But now we can look back on that and say, "I did it!"

Did you parent a toddler? We did, and that was quite a challenge. It was full of joyous and hard moments. Our daily happenings included chasing the runner we could not catch and cleaning up spoonfuls of mashed avocado, not to mention dealing with our toddlers' inability to control inappropriate impulses. Among the electrical outlets, coffee tables, stairways, and sidewalks, the accident traps around every corner seemed overwhelming. But we did it. We made it through. Not only did we make it through, but our children are healthier, stronger, and felt loved because we were there. We have been guiding our children all along the way.

Did you parent a preteen or teenager? Are you in the midst of it right now? This is another major stage of parenting that might be difficult. It feels a bit like parenting a giant toddler all over again, but now we catch glimpses of the young adult they will soon become. Between the arguing and eye-rolling, we get to have deep conversations about life and relationships. We have opportunities to explain to our children the hard decisions they will one day face. The conversations change over time—the parenting styles may change as well—yet we still guide our children, love them, and support them as they continue to grow up.

It's likely that most of us have had to work at becoming the parents we are today. We experiment with what works for our unique children. We utilize instinctual tools and recommendations from books, articles, and friends. Most of us already teach the most important stuff: character, ethics, teamwork, responsibility, core beliefs, family traditions, and much more. We do this with unconditional love because we are the parents. We are the loving parents. Our children's hopes and dreams are our hopes and dreams. Our children's successes and joys bring us our greatest joys.

Our children, whether they are two, twelve, or twenty years old, will push back against our guidance when they want different things than we do. They make different choices than we would. But we still parent them, even when it's hard and we aren't sure of the right answer. We parent even when we fail; failure is an opportunity for growth. We learn and do better because of that. And we do it, not because we are all qualified in the psychology of parenting philosophies and studies, but because we love our children and we want what we think is best for them. And that is good enough.

Homeschooling can be just another aspect of your parenting. No one is a perfect parent all the time, nor will you be a perfect homeschooler all the time. When we think back on our own homeschooling experiences, we see failures and successes. The picture of success that immediately pops into Mandi's head is her three children wearing their pajamas, laughing together around the kitchen table, while toying with silly wording for stories they wrote. She remembers rejoicing with her youngest daughter when she wrote the alphabet in cursive for the first time after months of struggle. Jessica remembers the days of snuggling with her newborn son while reading aloud to her six-year-old and giggling over the silly way the Big Friendly Giant speaks. She thinks of the conversations in the car after listening to an audiobook on a family road trip. While those memories are wonderful, we have had hard moments too. Moments where we've all cried, especially during the times we made the mistake of forcing lessons when our children weren't ready or willing. Some days, we lose our patience over the smallest things and go to bed at night with regret. It's not all sunshine; we have gloomy moments too. But we gratefully take the rain if it means we get rainbows as well.

This is the foundation we rely on, and it is the foundation of this book. If you are considering homeschooling, you are considering parenting your child through their character development *and* their academics. You want to be there for all of it. We understand you have hesitations. "I don't know what I'm doing!" "How will they make friends?" "How will they be equipped with emotional intelligence?" "Will I survive being with my kids all day?" "I don't want to fail my children." "Do I know enough to teach my teens and prepare them for college?" We wrote this book to answer these tough questions and remove your hesitation, because the choice to homeschool your family can be a beautiful and effective one.

We know you have kids to raise, errands to run, and life to live. We wrote this practical guide with you in mind. Each chapter addresses one common concern and can be read on its own to answer your hesitation. You don't need to read this guide cover to cover. Review the table of contents and start with the chapters addressing your biggest hesitations. Then come back to additional chapters for answers to other questions you may have.

- Part I addresses you and your capabilities. We flip the script and show you the capabilities that you didn't know you have or will have. If you think you cannot homeschool because of your inexperience, educational level, personality, or budget—think again!

- Part II tackles the fear of missing out on traditional school opportunities and experiences. Many people have the fear-of-missing-out (FOMO) plague, but we have the cure with ideas for opportunities and memory-making experiences that may feel like gifts to you, your children, and your family.

- Part III meets the major challenges families face when homeschooling. Making friends, getting into college, teaching unique learners, working full time while homeschooling, and finding community are some of the biggest concerns we consistently hear about. We dive in with stats and insights that can help you make the best decision for your family.

- A "can-do assessment" is available at the end of each chapter to help you evaluate your ability to homeschool. You don't need to check all the boxes. If you check off a couple of the items on the list, you can do this.

- In the Appendices, we help you with our Quick Start Guide, because you can do it! The Quick Start Guide provides six simple steps with ideas to help you begin your homeschool journey.

- Check out the glossary where we define homeschooling terms, such as *traditional schools*, *education*, and *deschooling*.

About Us

We are two veteran homeschool parents: Jessica is mom to a middle school daughter and elementary-age son, and Mandi is mom to two middle schoolers and an elementary-age daughter. Our past experiences and education have equipped us to write this guide, while our passions, struggles, and fun ideas have made it inspiring, honest, and practical.

Jessica left public school in seventh grade and was homeschooled until college. She knows firsthand how life-giving homeschooling can be—it gave her the ability to direct her educational future and the gift of time to pursue her passions in music and dance. She has worked with children for twenty years as a dance educator and has studied child development.

Mandi was a traditional school student throughout her entire formal education and thrived in that setting. As a former junior high school teacher, with a degree in school counseling and a master's degree in education, she understands the enriching experiences that can be offered in the traditional school environment.

We first met when our little girls danced together when they were almost three years old. As families, we connected through our shared passion for homeschooling. Currently, we partner together as co-authors, podcasters, and consultants for all things homeschooling. Together we have led a homeschool group of up to eighteen families for six years. Both of us have homeschooled our children by choice and with gratitude. The two of us together represent the knowledge and experience needed to approach this guide with balance and expertise.

Along with some helpful research, we share our adventures and others' experiences, lessons learned, and wisdom from our homeschooling journeys. Though we conceived, outlined, and edited this book together, most chapters were written by one or the other of us and reflect that person's point of view. We name the author at the beginning of each chapter. We both write with the same hope and conviction.

We love homeschooling our children and have experienced the wonder and struggle, the joy and difficulty, and the fun and freedom that it has to offer. We want the same for you.

I Want to Homeschool, but What If . . .

"Two roads diverged in a wood, and I—
I took the one less traveled by,
And that has made all the difference."

—ROBERT FROST

"I want to homeschool, but . . ." There are many ways people complete this sentence. Feeling inadequate or ill-equipped is a challenge. Making a change is hard. Doing something that feels against the grain is scary. Maybe a small nudge, a little reframing, and some evidence to the contrary can provide the answers you need to feel confident to homeschool. In part I, we want to eliminate common capability concerns to make homeschooling more accessible to all. If you can find your confidence to take that first step, you might just embark on the adventure you have only dreamed about.

Chapter 1

I Want to Homeschool, but What If I Don't Know the Content?

MANDI

"I want to homeschool, but I don't know the content." Let this sink in: you don't need to know the content. Doesn't make sense, does it? Knowing the content of what you are teaching *seems* like a super important element for educating your children, but this chapter is about shifting your mindset.

Have you ever said, "I have no idea what that means"? "How do I do an experiment?" "Does *i* come before *e* or the other way around?" Almost all of us have asked questions like these—and for some of us, this lack of knowledge makes us hesitant to homeschool. If this is you, keep reading.

We propose a mindset shift: You don't need to know the content before you teach it. With homeschooling, you can learn at the same time as your children. But we understand—teaching something you don't know much about can be scary.

Last year, when I was teaching the history of ancient civilizations to my kids, I had a huge light-bulb moment. Who knew that Mesopotamia and Ancient Egypt were completely different places? Not me! I thought they were the exact same location and the difference was that one simply preceded the other in time. I realized my error quickly as I read the script provided by our curriculum. My kids' eyes bulged, and we all chuckled at my bewilderment. Our camaraderie grew in that moment as I learned with them. Being educators doesn't mean knowing everything; it's a part of the parenting journey to help children learn how to learn and to enjoy learning together. That may be one of the most exciting parts of homeschooling!

Here's what you need to remember: no one has all the answers . . . not even the experts. When I was teaching junior high at a traditional school, I was in a continual state of learning my subjects. I was quite embarrassed when one of my eighth grade students asked, "Why are you reading the poster?" It was because I did not know the eight parts of speech by memory. There was a lot to know, and I told her so.

Most educators are in the same boat—even the trained, experienced ones. In addition, it can be difficult to teach the content while also helping children learn how to think and how to learn. It's good for our children and it's good for us to develop thinking skills, but it's hard to know what those are sometimes. But there are tools to help. It's important to keep in mind that every type of professional is constantly learning and relies on tools for their trade. There are three tools almost every professional teacher and homeschool parent use to educate students or their own children when it comes to content and knowing the subject: curriculum, enrichment, and personal experiences.

Let's start off with what almost every educator uses, whether they are in a classroom-based school or home school: curriculum.

Helpful Tool #1: Curriculum

Curriculum is basically what we teach our children, which includes planned educational lessons and activities. It's a collection of information found in books, media, experiences, and activities related to a subject that aid in teaching students important skills and knowledge over a length of time. Curriculum study plans can span a week, a month, a year, and even longer. Some curriculum includes formal assessments, but we can also informally assess our children's understanding of those subjects. Curriculum can be faith-based or secular, online or print, and can align with a variety of educational philosophies or approaches.

Types of Curriculum Content

The following types of curriculum show the wide range of options available to homeschoolers. Choices include deciding between faith-based and secular content, grade-based and mastery-based levels, comprehensive study or a singular focus, and project-based or problem-solving activities.

- Faith-based content—curriculum that includes content centered around a faith-based worldview.
- Secular content—curriculum that includes content centered around a secular worldview.
- Grade-level—curriculum that is labeled with a grade level and includes content typical for the indicated level based on educational standards.
- Mastery-based—curriculum that is focused on mastering a specific set of skills or information and is not labeled for a specific grade level.
- Comprehensive—curriculum that is comprehensive in its coverage of a subject.
- Singular focus and exposure—curriculum that provides exposure to a singular topic within a subject.
- Project-based activities—curriculum that focuses on learning content through working on a project to complete a final product.
- Problem-based activities—curriculum where learners primarily solve stand-alone problems using worksheets.

Curriculum Components and Packaging

Curriculum can be packaged differently depending on its objectives.

- Boxed/all-in-one curriculum—this curriculum comes in a single box, including all the core academic subjects for a grade level delivered through textbooks, workbooks, assessment booklets, and reference or enrichment books. Sometimes this is referred to as an "open-and-go" curriculum, if it provides everything you need in one curriculum and you do not need to prepare ahead of time to present the material.

- Single-subject curriculum—Each subject stands on its own and is bought separately as a workbook, textbook, and/or reference book. Materials for the different subjects can come from different publishers.

- Unit studies—a topic of interest exposes students to content and skills from multiple subjects. Students study the topic using a variety of curriculum components, reference books, digital media, and experiential learning. Unit studies can be delivered digitally for viewing and printing, or through workbooks and reference books.

- Supplemental curriculum (i.e., workbooks and manuals)—this type of curriculum provides opportunities for more practice or to dive more deeply into a subject or topic. This curriculum can include reference books, craft boxes, and kits to enrich the learning experience.

- Online—these curriculum programs include written materials, videos, and assessments delivered through an app or website program.

The Advantages of Curriculum

One of the useful things about many curriculum programs is that they include a teacher's manual with scripts for the content, discussion questions for analyzing the content, and—the best part—an answer key. The content is laid out for parents in the teacher's manual, and the content and activities are laid out for students in the student workbook.

There are various types of curriculum, so if your children are not thriving with one type, there are others to choose from that may be a better fit for your children's interests and abilities. You can decide to go with a grade-level curriculum each year, or pick a mastery-based curriculum and move forward where your children's progress takes you, without grade-level designations. The choice is yours, and it's awesome to have a choice.

Typically, curriculum is a very popular tool educators use for content, and it is extremely helpful. If you do not know the content, we highly recommend using curriculum.

What an Eight-Year-Old Thinks

I asked my daughter Maisy what she liked about homeschooling, and she shared this with me: "I liked the *Mrs. Wordsmith Storytellers Word a Day* book, where every day we would learn words like *swagger, mesmerizing, greedy,* and *perplexed.* I like going to SeaWorld® and LEGOLAND® and there were not much people there. I like doing the 'stations' when you teach or read to us—where we would have a station with water beads to stick our hands in and wiggle around and try to find the items, and a station for Star Wars Day and we played with fun putty and made it into stars. I like when we did the *Musicals* book, and then we watched *Shrek, The Greatest Showman, Aladdin,* and *Hamilton.* I really like the theme days, like 'May the 4th be with you' (Star Wars Day) and Harry Potter Days."

Helpful Tool #2: Enrichment

What Is Enrichment?

Enrichment is anything that enhances the quality or value of education. Enrichment can be a pursuit of our own interests (our heritage, life skills, etc.) and our children's interests while embellishing the formal curriculum for a particular topic. It's the spice of homeschooling!

Charlotte, mother of five children, enrolled her youngest two daughters in classes to learn Hula dancing, an important part of her ethnic heritage. She shared this with me: "Hula is more than just entertainment, it's a beautiful, graceful form of dance where my girls have learned concentration and balance. The dance tells a story with the soothing melodies and lyrics that focus on love, nature, and life."

Johnny, age thirteen, wants to become a Grandmaster (the highest title awarded by the International Chess Federation), so he goes weekly to his local library's chess club to play with other children and adults of all ages, expertise, and backgrounds. As a homeschooling teen, he has the time to spend hours daily on chess.com competing with people from around the world. Johnny shared this with me: "Chess is a great way to exercise the mind. The beauty of chess is when you lose a game, there was no luck involved. It's all about the study and practice you put in."

We organize enrichment into three categories and recommend trying an activity from each one when getting started: adventures, read-alouds and audiobooks, and other types.

Adventures

Adventures are what many call "field trips"—but they are so much more. Adventures are experiences that feed the soul. Well-established research demonstrates that experiences are a critical way people of all ages learn (Kolb 2015). The idea that children are learning all the time through experiencing the world around them releases us from needing to be in books all day. Whether we are traveling the world or going to our neighborhood playground, every outing offers an opportunity for learning.

Here are different types of adventures:

- Content enrichment experiences—Take a topic of interest and head to a place that enhances what you are learning: a museum, factory, nature trail, recreation center, or library. When we studied Claude Monet, we adventured to the lily pad pond at Balboa Park in San Diego, where my children each created their own Monet-inspired lily pad painting. Other times we study nature by taking hikes and talking about the trees, plants, and insects along the way.

- Stand-alone journeys—This is when we take a break from the routine and go on a journey. We had a blast with our children and their friends going on a donut road trip to multiple donut shops. We learned how donuts were made, sang donut songs, read donut picture books, and rated each donut on taste, texture, and overall experience. Our children made charts and learned that not all donuts or donut shops were created equal. This stand-alone adventure was, simply put, delicious.

- Enrichment organized by others—Some organizations exist solely to take us on an awesome, educationally-curated adventure. Try a web search for "homeschool field trips in [your state or city]." Join local homeschool Facebook groups to find field trips, hiking clubs, and other planned adventures. Some regions have companies that organize and facilitate field trips for homeschoolers, but you may need to search more widely to find trips near you.

- Explore with a Co-op—Another option is to join a cooperative (co-op) composed of homeschool families. Co-ops can be found through friends of friends, teammates, social media groups, and more (see chapter 9). Co-ops come in many forms. Some of them are organized purely for homeschool parents to take turns designing educational experiences to enjoy together. Our co-op organized a field trip to a camel dairy, where we toured the dairy, sampled camel milk lotion, and even rode camels!

Pairing adventures with content can really enhance their impact on everyone involved. For us, it's this combination that makes a joy-filled, memory-making moment while establishing the connection between content and real life.

Read-Alouds and Audiobooks

We love read-alouds! Reading aloud to our children is one of parenting's finest privileges. The discussions and discoveries that arise naturally from a storyline are an engaging way to teach a particular topic and grow our children's characters. Reading aloud offers organic opportunities to safely introduce mature topics and parent our children through them. We can read aloud to our children while they dig in the playground sandbox, cuddle with us on the couch, or play with slime or toy cars.

My husband has read aloud to our children almost daily for the past six years using book series he enjoys, such as Harry Potter, The Vanderbeekers, and The Wingfeather Saga. He shared, "As a dad who misses school time during the day while I am working, I love reading aloud to my children because it is an activity I can share with all of my kids regardless of their varied interests. I enjoy the opportunities read-alouds offer—to discuss shared human experiences, emotions, and challenges with my children as we encounter different people, places, and cultures—both real and imagined—together."

Listening to audiobooks (free to borrow on public library apps), either together or individually, is an enriching way to fill time when riding the bus, in the car, or hanging out while big brother plays soccer. My kids and I often listen to audiobooks on a Bluetooth speaker when I need to fold laundry, wash the dishes, or rest my eyes from a migraine. Some of our favorites have been *Pollyanna*, *Wonder*, and *The Trumpet of the Swan.* Introducing audiobooks and read-alouds makes reading accessible to children who struggle with reading independently but enjoy stories.

Some of the most treasured connecting moments in our family are our read-aloud times.

Other Enrichment

In homeschooling, content delivery can happen in multiple ways far beyond textbooks and lectures. It's the stuff our kids look forward to receiving in the mail or the opportunity to try and test ideas with their own hands. Whether at home or out and about, enrichment mixes education and life experiences to build an interactive context for the information our kids want to learn.

At Home

Magazines, screen time (e.g., museum websites, games, apps, how-to videos), craft kits, and subject-based subscription boxes are fun ways to deliver content while engaging your children's interests. We list some ideas here that our children enjoy.

- Websites like National Geographic Kids, the Getty, and the Smithsonian host curated talks and informational and demonstration videos.
- YouTube channels such as Operation Ouch and Mr. DeMaio teach science. The educational websites ABCmouse and IXL teach grade-level content. My son plays the *F1 Manager* video game, which teaches him about car parts and budgeting.

- A weekly subscription magazine, *The Week Junior* is an age-appropriate magazine where children (and adults too) read about the world's current events, learn about new books, and solve word puzzles.
- My tween daughter gladly spends her free time illustrating books she has written using Canva, a free graphic design website.
- My eight-year-old and I spent two delightful hours one school day learning embroidery together, using a kit that provided access to free, online instructional videos, developing a new lifelong skill for both of us.
- A monthly subscription to hands-on kits is another option. My son received and assembled kits for a walking robot and a hydraulic claw from Tinker Crate (KiwiCo).

Out and About

Organizations that provide lessons, laboratory courses, internship opportunities, and passion-inspired classes can be especially helpful as students progress and the content becomes more advanced. Research what's available in your region before making any big decisions.

- Search for organizations using terms like "homeschool science lab classes" or "homeschool art classes near me" to get started.
- Many large cities offer free homeschool classes and enrichment programs for kids through their recreation and parks programs, such as martial arts, violin and ukulele lessons, fashion design, Ballet Folklórico, animation, and more. Search "free lessons for kids in [your nearest major city]."
- Check out kidsoutandabout.com, which serves dozens of cities, for more enrichment opportunities.

One of these enrichments might be the very thing that sparks your child's lifelong passion.

Mix It Up

Screen time can spark a truly memorable learning experience. One evening, my spouse was watching a documentary about Bethany Hamilton, the young surfer who lost an arm after being attacked by a shark. My children's passionate interest became the inspiration for our next week of school time. We read aloud Hamilton's *Soul Surfer*, watched how-to-surf videos, played at the beach, viewed National Geographic Kids shark videos, and then visited the surf museum in San Diego. Bethany Hamilton's surfboard with a shark bite taken out of it was on exhibit! Research what's around you and take advantage of the opportunities within reach.

Here's something to try: Does your child love riding elevators? If there's an elevator nearby, that can be an engineering lesson in the making. Watch videos on YouTube about the mechanics of the machines or about famous elevators around the world, read library books with elevator stories and histories, write your own story after taking an elevator ride, and invite a few friends to join in to make a memorable homeschool day. Utilizing the various ways your children may receive information can make a big difference in connecting their hearts and minds to content so that they truly learn it.

No matter where you live, there's a mix of ways to learn about history, art, engineering, mathematics, and more that can fill up your children's curiosity cups. Some homeschoolers focus mostly on enrichment to deliver content, while others use it sparingly. The beauty of homeschooling is that the choice is yours.

Helpful Tool #3: You—Your Personal Values and Experiences

There is one more tool you can use to educate your children when it comes to content and knowing the subject: you can give them *you*. You are filled with decades of life experience, know-how, and values. Share that with your children. Homeschooling is a special opportunity not just to impart knowledge about academic subjects, but to impart your heart on all the subjects. Your home culture, vision, mission, beliefs, character, life lessons, experiences, celebrations, approach to challenges, and more—give those to your children.

The following are ways my husband and I weave our personal values and experiences into our family life:

- We practice our customs with our children through role-playing, like appropriate ways of greeting members of our family and community.

It can be ridiculously fun to role-play the wrong way too (among safe participants).

- Since my family is a faith-based family, we explore religious beliefs by learning the history, symbolism, and practices of religions, and celebrating together even if it's not the actual holiday date. This helps the holiday mean more to our children.

- Using table talk questions to talk about our favorite childhood traditions, practices, foods, and learning moments makes dinner together special for us. We've made recipes together and shared our favorite dishes from our past.

- Playing our favorite board games and teaching my tried-and-true strategies makes for a nostalgic skill-building time together.

- We watch meaningful movies and documentaries and read picture books together that share the difficulties or discrimination we (or people we know) have faced and discuss what we learned. (See chapter 10 for more.)

Many families share the homeschooling load with co-parents, grandparents, friends, and others, often sharing responsibilities in unexpected ways. Families frequently designate one parent as the primary educator responsible for homeschooling, while the other family members augment homeschooling lessons with their passions and skills. Here are some examples:

- Cody, homeschooling dad of two children, is a history buff, and when his family talks history, he fills in intriguing details and fascinating stories that the curriculum may have left out.

- Grandma Teri loves writing and shares that love through editing and discussing the books her tween granddaughter has authored.

- Farzad, homeschooling dad of two children, is dedicated to playing sports and volunteered to teach basketball and sportsmanship as a coach in his son's basketball league.

- Aunt Leslie, a vegan chef, taught her homeschooled niece Amy how to make macaroni and cheese and other favorite foods the vegan way.

- Jake, Jessica's husband, loves *Dungeons & Dragons* and attends a weekly session with his friends. He is currently teaching his two children to play and will be leading our co-op's D&D club.

- Grandma Keeley teaches her two homeschooled grandchildren the responsibility of caring for her chickens. They practice fractions as they bake together, they learn household skills, and they are currently creating mosaic tile art using the walls of their fire pit.

- Jason, homeschooling dad of five children, shared his engineering skills when he asked his eleven-year-old son (who is a landscaping enthusiast) to help him design the irrigation system for their yard. They dug ditches and laid pipes and sprinklers themselves. His older kids call it "Daddy School" when he teaches them math and Bible lessons.

- Grandpa Steve helps his three grandchildren put together their MEL Science physics kits, sharing his aerospace engineering skills.

- John, homeschooling dad of four children, is passionate about financial matters and teaches investment skills every Sunday when he hands his children their hard-earned allowances.

- Grandma Mimi, a former piano teacher, came out of retirement to teach weekly lessons to her three grandchildren.

- Grauntie (great-aunt) Jo Lyn finds delight in caring for her homeschooled great-nieces and -nephews and acts as a "Homeschool Assistant" to their mom, taking them to co-op events, where she engages with them in their learning activities.

- Marcus, my husband, needed help replacing our bathroom toilets. He invited our ten-year-old son to learn with him on YouTube, and they successfully replaced two toilets!

Give yourself to your children, not just because you are an expert in and care about your personal values and experiences, but because, when it comes to building stronger relationships and strengthening family ties, your values and perspectives are what matter most.

Sibling Support

Jeanine, homeschool parent and travel agent, California

Jeanine, a homeschool parent of six children with a fourteen-year age span, shared ways that her older children have helped educate their siblings. She said, "The sweetest thing homeschooling brings to us are the bonds and friendships built between siblings and parent/child. This is something that only time spent together can grow."

- Chores: "After my first ones knew what was expected of them and how to do chores, the next kids followed suit without much effort."

- Surfing: "In high school and college it's sweet to see our older daughter encouraging her sisters to wake up early and hit the waves. Sweet bonding time."

- Love of cooking and service: "Kids learn by doing. As the older kids watch me cook and serve others, they start to help the younger ones (who want to be a part of the action) do the same. Pretty soon the older ones take the reins. It's sweet now to see my nineteen-year-old son calling his six-year-old sister to come down to help cook and make a new recipe."

- Skateboarding: "My eldest convinced the kids to pool their money together to buy a used skate ramp. They all worked to disassemble it and rebuild it in our front yard. The teens and little ones now enjoy skating together and hanging out at night after a long day of activities."

There are many ways to find content for different ages and grade levels. For some people, homeschooling becomes more intimidating as our children get older and the content becomes more complicated and advanced (see chapters 15 and 16). But through curriculum, enrichment, and ourselves, homeschooling can be full of curiosity and wonder, with lots of interesting content. We can saturate our children's lives with what's important, infusing topics with our own passions and values. It's okay when we don't know the content; this can actually be a gift to us—because now we get to grow our enthusiasm with our children, learn with them, and spark joy for each other as we explore the unknown. Go discover together!

Can-Do Assessment for Knowing the Content

- ❏ I feel comfortable asking teachers, friends, and other homeschool parents what curriculum they use. I feel comfortable researching options (using websites like homeschoolcurriculumreview.com or a trusted publisher referred to me by another parent or teacher).

- ❏ I can read up on content that is interesting to my child or me and share it with my child.

- ❏ I have time and space for organizing an enriching adventure (museums, parks, cultural centers, factories, and so on) once a month.

- ❏ I can organize group events. If not, I have friends who like to organize or plan events that I would feel comfortable asking to join.

- ❏ I feel comfortable reading aloud picture books and chapter books to my children (all ages). As I read, I can think of broader topics to discuss with my children organically.

- ❏ I know (or I can start exploring) my child's interests. I am able to research a book, class, subscription box, activity, or lesson, or even create a themed day for my child to dive more deeply into a topic of interest.

- ❏ I (or my family members) have skills or interests that I can offer my child. I feel comfortable teaching these skills or interests.

- ❏ I can explore what I am passionate about and share that with my child.

Chapter 2

I Want to Homeschool, but What If I Don't Know How to Teach?

MANDI

Many people think that they don't know how to teach and are overwhelmed by the idea of becoming their children's primary educator. We hear this concern frequently from people we know and even the random people we meet. "I don't know how to teach," or "I don't know the first thing about teaching," or "That's awesome you homeschool, but I don't know how I would teach *my* kids." Ready for another mindset shift? You already teach your children! You have been teaching them their whole lives, and you've likely been successful at it.

We understand the implied meaning to be, "I am not trained like a credentialed teacher," but there are many ways to be and become successful at teaching. You already know how to teach *your* specific child. You have been teaching your child since the moment you met them, and your child has been teaching you *how* to teach them. As your child grew, you grew too. During this time, you both have been observing each other, testing boundaries, trying new skills, and experimenting with your roles as parent and child, as well as teacher and student. You have been doing this for years; it is a lifelong process. This mutual learning is called "parenting." We hear from naysayers and supporters alike how teachers and parents are two different groups of people. They aren't! In the traditional school context, it's true, but when it comes to raising kids, parents are their teachers in immeasurable ways. One of the most important aspects of parenting is guiding and teaching your children to prepare them for life. You teach them daily. But if you are worried about not having a college degree or formal training in teaching, read on.

I Don't Have a Teaching Credential

You do not need one. Yes, a classroom teacher needs a credential and the education that comes with it; there is specific training that is helpful when one is teaching in a traditional school. But *you* do not need a credential. You are not teaching twenty to thirty students whom you had never met before the first day of school. You are not teaching a classroom of students equipped with different skill sets, from different home cultures, with various interests, and with a variety of special needs. You are teaching only *your* children, who you know better than any other people in the world. You already have years of experience teaching your unique children. In fact, when it comes to your children, you have a life credential.

I Don't Have a College Degree

Your children do not need you to have a college degree or a degree in education. While recent homeschooling research is pretty sparse, historic studies nationwide found that homeschool students from "families with low income and in which the parents have little education are scoring, on average, above state-school averages . . . In addition, the most recent research on homeschooling shows that the parents' teacher-certification has little to no relationship with their children's academic achievement" (Ray 2004, 6). You can use tools like curriculum, online research, tutors, and outsourced college prep courses to explore and learn necessary information; you do not need to have every answer on the tip of your tongue. When I was teaching junior high, many times my students asked me questions and I had to say, "I will get back to you on that tomorrow." Then, I used available tools and returned the next day with a new learning experience and knowledge from which we all grew. Now, as a homeschool parent, I can say, "I don't know. Let's find the answer together!"

Close Relationships Are Critical to the Learning Process

In today's North American society, the norm is that a credentialed person outside of the family teaches a group of students of the same age in a traditional school structure that hasn't changed much in a century. However, this does not mean it is the better way. It's time to remember who our children most frequently connect with, look up to, and desire to be with on a daily basis. Even if there are struggles and challenges between parents and their children, connection with loving parents is what children desperately want and most need.

Family support or parent involvement in a child's education is hailed as one of the top predictors in school success throughout transitional kindergarten to twelfth grade, whether it be through motivational encouragement, field trip attendance, room parent assistance, or even helping with homework (Lansford 2020). The American Psychological Association's report "Top 20 Principles from Psychology for Early Childhood Teaching and Learning" states that "interpersonal relationships and communication are critical to both the teaching-learning process and the social development of children" (2019, 27). Parents are typically the adults with whom our children have the closest relationships. Can we imagine any better person for the critical job of educating them? We have been building our interpersonal relationship and learning to communicate with each other since day one. Though sometimes we need outside help with parent-child relationship skills, we are the most important relationship in our children's lives. Spending positive, connection-building time together gives us that special knowledge to meet and address our children's needs, interests, struggles, and quirks in ways that best suit them.

Teaching Teens

Emily, homeschool parent for thirteen years with three boys, Georgia and New England

We asked homeschoolers across the United States what they love best about homeschooling their teenagers. Emily shared: "My kids have never stopped hanging out with us—my oldest is twenty-four years old now. He was homeschooled from sixth grade on. (When I started homeschooling I knew only three people who homeschooled and was scared silly.) And even though we live on either end of the east coast, he texts me every day and calls two to three times a week, just to talk. My fifteen-year-old twins just told me last weekend that I haven't been spending much time with them lately, and they asked if we could watch a few movies together—and I teach three classes with them every day. My kids are begging for more of my time, which is the best part of homeschooling if you ask me."

You Already Are an Experienced Teacher for Your Child

Maybe you figured out that your child needed white noise, a story, or special music to fall asleep at bedtime. Maybe you demonstrated how to pump your legs on the swings at the playground. Who taught your children how to do the laundry and fold their clothes? Can your children put on socks, play *Uno* or other card games, make toast, set the table, or play a pretend game with friends? Somehow, your children learned how to speak up for their needs, wait their turn to get their hair styled, hang up clothes in a dressing room, and show kind manners to the waitstaff at a favorite restaurant. Likely your children learned most of those skills with you. You can teach your children, and you've been doing it for years. When I was a rookie classroom teacher, I relied heavily upon my students' parents for insight and partnership, because I knew the parents were the experts about their children and were more experienced than me. A classroom teacher may have a teaching credential, but you have a Ph.D. in your child.

You Can Develop Your Teaching Skills

You can earn your own unofficial, self-certified credential in whatever you want these days—that includes teaching. Even though the content, learning styles, and educational philosophies can be overwhelming at first, you can learn. You can start off slowly and then gradually build the skills and knowledge you need. Between homeschooling conferences, webinars, books, podcasts, online articles, and discussions with other homeschool parents, there's plenty of information available for free or a small fee. You can also study various homeschooling approaches, such as Charlotte Mason, classical education, unschooling, and more (see the glossary for definitions).

Here are ways to develop and enhance your teaching delivery:

- Watch curriculum-provided how-to videos.
- Attend a teacher's training session for curriculum when offered (online or in-person), which will give ideas and model ways to teach the material.
- Read the teacher's guides and scripts until you are comfortable delivering the content.
- Practice some problems and answer a few questions in the student workbooks yourself to become more familiar with the process and answers.

Plan on spending a specific amount of time per week, maybe one to four hours, on these ideas to build your own skills.

Your Child Will Learn, Even without You

Since the moment your child learned to suck their thumb in the womb or could identify your voice, they have been learning on their own. Learning is a natural need for human beings. Developmental psychologist Peter Gray explains that "we adults can help them best not by teaching, but by making sure that they have adequate social and physical environments and time and space in which to explore" (Gray 2016, para. 3). When we provide the free time and the space, resources, and tools, as well as our help when requested, our children may learn more readily or even more deeply by engaging in their own explorations. Some kids can even design their own curriculum about a topic that interests them.

If you still think that you cannot teach your child, then consider being your child's guide. As parents, we can guide our children in their learning, provide direction, give encouragement, and inspire deep dives into their interests. Your children will learn in this way too. Your guidance can set their course.

As homeschool parents, we get to continue to do what we've done since our children's days in infancy. As Gray put it, children are born to learn: "Children are biologically predisposed to take charge of their own education" (Gray 2013, 6). This is powerful in that we only need to create an environment for learning and provide the tools our children need. Sharing our enthusiasm, along with creativity and acceptance, may just be the key to teaching them.

Designing Their Own Curriculum

Valorie, veteran homeschool parent and high school English teacher for a homeschool community, Connecticut

Valorie, homeschool parent of five children, has homeschooled her children for twenty-five years and just graduated her last two children (twins!). She shared this with me: "I let my kids design their curriculum; it's probably the best thing I did for them in high school. One of my kids designed a prototype of a sustainable building that produces enough food for all the residents in the building and has zero emissions—and then brought it with her to her urban design class in college. I never would have come up with that myself."

Feeling Inadequate and Unqualified

Teri, retired homeschool parent and grandparent of two homeschooled kids

Teri shared: "If you have a child that has been in traditional school and now you are hesitant to homeschool . . . You can do this. My daughter had been in traditional school for seven years. She and I decided that at the end of sixth grade she'd be homeschooled. The hurdle that I had to clear was the feeling that I was not qualified to teach my daughter. I barely graduated high school; algebra was not my forte. My daughter had been a straight-A student in school with a strong aptitude for math. I was terrified that I would ruin my daughter's education, but as it turned out, my daughter helped me understand beginning algebra, at the same time increasing her algebra skills. Learning together was remarkable."

Can-Do Assessment to Feel Confident Teaching My Child

- ☐ I can make a list of skills, subjects, activities, and character-building lessons that I have already taught my child.

- ☐ I can make a list of my child's strengths, abilities, and areas needing growth.

- ☐ I can make a list of what I think I can teach or guide my child in over the next twelve weeks.

- ☐ I can name one resource to learn from in the next month to develop myself as a homeschool parent (e.g., conference, webinar, book, podcast, internet article, or discussion with a homeschooling friend or seasoned educator).

- ☐ I can identify my child's interests and provide access to resources (books, courses, online resources, supplies or materials, etc.) for my child to pursue their interests on their own.

Chapter 3

I Want to Homeschool, but What If My Child Won't Learn from Me?

JESSICA

We know that moment of panic when we feel like our child just doesn't want to learn from us. It's frustrating! It feels impossible sometimes. It can be easy to think that it's best for your child to learn from someone else.

Let that moment pass, because you have an entire life to coach them, not just one lesson, day, or week.

I am going to reiterate a familiar point here: if you taught your child to walk, talk, or use a spoon, your child *can* learn from you (see chapter 2). Has every teaching moment gone smoothly? Of course not. In the process of raising littles, did some of us feel like we were going to lose our minds? Yes, we did. Think about the toddler phase and those fiercely independent children who wanted no help from anyone. They could and would do it themselves! We still feel those moments in our souls. Sometimes our children got frustrated at the learning process, but eventually they mastered the desired skill and all parties felt the accomplishment. Those moments were hard but grew easier with time. We look back now and are thankful we were there, *with* our children in their early stages of walking, talking, and using a spoon . . . and that's what mattered.

Homeschooling Scenarios

It's natural as you consider homeschooling to worry that your children won't learn from you; there's no comprehensive manual on homeschooling (or parenting) the children you are given. However, identifying reasons your children may be resistant to learning from you or with you is critical to knowing how to address them. The problem may be a behavioral or discipline issue, it may be a matter of interest, or it may be a more challenging issue that needs to be addressed with professional help. For your encouragement, we offer the following scenarios that describe different types of learners and situations where homeschooling can help your child learn from you without squashing their spirit.

Scenario 1: Learners Who Are Strong-Willed and Independent

What It Looks Like

Some children maintain the independence that served them so well in toddlerhood. And though that has the potential to serve them well in adulthood, it can be a challenge for parents. These children may want to control whether they sit or stand to learn, to control how long they want to focus on learning, or to teach the content to themselves.

How Homeschooling Can Help

Homeschooling can give us the flexibility to empower those future leaders to make some decisions regarding their learning. Perhaps we let our children choose the schedule for the day. Maybe our children would like to look at a lesson plan and decide for themselves how to accomplish the objectives. Going one step further, maybe they would like to learn a lesson independently or from a sibling. Involving our children may help them feel ownership and be more willing to participate in their learning. Homeschooling allows for autonomy, which plays a major role in developing a child's sense of self and is an opportunity for growth on their own terms. As the authors of *The Self-Driven Child* explain, "The brain develops according to how it's used. By giving your child the opportunity to make decisions for herself while still young, you will help her brain build the circuits that are necessary for resilience in the face of stress" (Stixrud and Johnson 2019, 37).

Mistakes We Made

Mandi

I had a rough time teaching my youngest daughter how to read. She wouldn't do her reading work when I asked, and the fatigue and frustration brought us both to conflict and tears. I knew that forcing my child went against my own personal convictions as a parent, and I felt like I was failing both my daughter and myself. But then I noticed that my daughter was delighted to learn from her older brother during their free play. So, I asked my son, who was ten years old at the time, to partner with his little sister in this reading endeavor; he happily helped when she needed it. They celebrated a joint accomplishment when she conquered her 100th reading vocabulary word. Now my son proudly shares that he taught his sister to read.

Scenario 2: Learners Who Are Anxious and Perfectionistic

What It Looks Like

For some personalities, demonstrating understanding can be riddled with anxiety; the pressure to perform can be very intense. I felt this a lot growing up. I had such a strong need to be perfect by getting every answer correct that I could not perform on the spot. Or I'd be the child crying when I got a 99 percent on a math quiz. I think the people pleasers of the world also fit into this group. Learning from someone you are eager to please can be highly challenging.

How Homeschooling Can Help

These children need space. They need space to process without pressure. Space to check their own answers before going through work together. Homeschooling can allow for the space and low-pressure environment these children need. If the situation is fraught with too much anxiety, outsourcing a portion of instruction may help; we offer some ideas for outsourcing later in this chapter.

Scenario 3: Learners Who Are Uninterested

What It Looks Like

An uninterested learner may complain a lot or immediately need a snack or bathroom break when it's time for learning. (Take a deep breath and grab another cup of coffee.) We wonder, "Why does my child get easily distracted or lose focus during a lesson even though they can build with toy bricks for two hours without a break?" This is extremely frustrating for parents and likely becomes frustrating for the child as well.

How Homeschooling Can Help

Being able to customize curriculum and plan adventures can help a lot. Because we are not locked into a specific curriculum, we can work to figure out what our children are interested in learning through observation and exposure.

Study your child. You can then pursue their interests through curriculum, adventures, and bonding experiences. Compromise can be another great tool in this scenario. If you have a child who is interested in outer space, find adventures, tools, books, a unit study, or science curriculum on space that will be fun and interesting for them. Then, leverage their learning enjoyment for that subject by first focusing on a math lesson for fifteen minutes. Bonus points for finding a way to make the math concepts space-related!

We all pay better attention and work more intently when we are interested. My family loves camping throughout the United States, and my children often pointed out the various sizes and colors of birds we saw. So one year, I decided we would spend time in a North American Birds unit study. At the end of the year, when I asked my five-year-old son what his favorite part of homeschooling is, he replied, "bird study!"

Scenario 4: Learners Who Think and Learn Differently

What It Looks Like

Teaching can sometimes feel like going in circles: we explain a concept, our children misunderstand, they ask a question that we, in turn, misunderstand, and over and over again. My daughter and I go through this circular confusion in math. Our brains are wired differently for numbers. I think I'm explaining a concept clearly and simply, but my daughter becomes upset and frustrated because it makes no sense to her.

How Homeschooling Can Help

Homeschooling allows us to change course or tactics at any point when things aren't working. If our goal is to raise lifelong learners, then learning shouldn't be frustrating—or else both parent and child will want to quit learning together. This is a battle that nobody wins, even if one of us gets our way. We must adapt to our children, figure out what the disconnect is, and find ways to alter the teaching.

For my daughter, I tried our math curriculum's instructional video that gives a three- to six-minute lesson for each chapter. My daughter not only had fun watching the video lessons, but finally understood the concepts. That video completely changed her attitude toward math. More importantly, we learned that we don't process information the same way, which grew our relationship and understanding of each other. Homeschooling has a double advantage: progress is not just academic, but interpersonal as well.

Scenario 5: Learners Who Feel Inadequate

What It Looks Like

This child feels like they can't or won't be able to learn. They may feel like a failure or like they are not smart enough to succeed. Sometimes children are hard on themselves without any external input. Often, though, children may have experienced bullying, shaming, or other negative responses that make them feel like they cannot learn. These children may become emotionally resistant to learning.

How Homeschooling Can Help

If our children are missing free throws and comparing themselves to kids scoring three-pointers, they are bound to feel inferior. In homeschooling, though, our children don't know if anyone is scoring any points at all! When we don't have anyone to compare ourselves to, we are less likely to feel like a failure. With homeschooling, we can move at a slower pace and spend our time coaching our children through difficult tasks.

If our children feel inadequate because they have been exposed to bullying or shaming by others, this can be remedied with homeschooling. At home, we can provide a positive learning environment and encourage our children's progress at a comfortable pace without intimidation or embarrassment.

Scenario 6: Learners Who Are Defiant and Difficult

What It Looks Like

Some children tend to refuse to do anything we ask. They may purposely break rules, refuse to follow instructions, or have bursts of anger when they perceive a situation is unfair or for no apparent reason at all.

How Homeschooling Can Help

This is one of the hardest situations for parents to face. Recommendations from occupational therapists and child development specialists typically include instituting consistent routines and rhythms for adding structure to this child's day and providing simple ways for them to make decisions about their own daily life. If the behavior seems to be beyond what you can navigate with familial support, there may be behavioral or neurological issues that need to be addressed. A pediatrician is an excellent place to start. They may recommend another professional, such as a family therapist, child psychologist, or occupational therapist. If a child is defiant at school, homeschooling may alleviate some of the consequences of that behavior at school. If a child is defiant toward their parent but seems willing to abide by rules and follow the instruction of others, homeschooling may indeed be challenging for both parties. In either case, seek the help of a qualified professional.

Scenario 7: Learners Who Don't Want a Parent to Teach Them

What It Looks Like

Some children say that their parent isn't the person they want to teach them. Maybe they have been in a traditional school and are accustomed to having a nonparent as their teacher. It's not the kind of relationship they are used to with their parent, and they don't want to make a change. This can be heartbreaking for the parent.

How Homeschooling Can Help

It sounds funny, but homeschooling itself can help with a child's resistance to homeschooling. Every new type of relationship requires time for adjusting and becoming familiar with new roles. Be patient with yourself and your child. Plan experiences together that make your presence the reason for the fun. Make it your job to be your best self during your intentional time together.

After you decide to homeschool, there is a necessary transition from the traditions of public school to the home school. Try taking some time, a few weeks or months, to recalibrate your mindsets when going from traditional schooling to homeschooling. This is called "deschooling." Though desks, worksheets, and precise schedules are needed in many traditional classrooms, they are not necessary when homeschooling. Allowing for this period of transition helps us recognize ingrained traditional school practices, and then retrain our brains to see education as a lifestyle without time boundaries or subject limits. The idea is to forget about typical traditional school schedules for a few weeks and just enjoy being present together. It should feel like summer break!

Scenario 8: Learners Who Don't Want to Be Homeschooled

What It Looks Like

Some children like attending traditional school and don't want to leave it. Parents may choose to homeschool for valid reasons, but these children can't see the decision from our perspective. They may resent us for even suggesting this change and won't listen to our reasoning.

Can Homeschooling Help?

Mandi and I think so! Time together can make a difference. You can spend time with your children and gently explore their reasoning. Ask them what they like about traditional school and what they would miss about it. What are they worried about or expecting to happen if they homeschool? Validate and address your children's concerns. Explain your reasons for wanting to homeschool, and create a vision for homeschooling together. Demonstrate that homeschooling life could be pretty great by finding educational ways to have fun together and celebrating the new things your children try or learn. Propose a trial period of homeschooling for a month, a semester, or a year, and then evaluate your collective experiences. Your child may be more willing to give this a try with less resistance.

A Teen Adapts to Homeschool

Jacob, homeschooled teen now homeschooling his children

After eighth grade, when his guardianship changed, Jacob was pulled from public school to begin homeschooling alongside his cousins. He shared, "For me, the most enjoyable aspect of public school was the relationships I had with my fellow students. I remember looking forward to our interactions waiting at the bus stop, walking through the halls, and eating in the cafeteria every day.

"When I learned that I would be moving to another state and would be homeschooled after the eighth grade, the thought of missing out on these public school interactions made me sad and angry. I treasured the friendships I had and truly enjoyed spending time with my peers, and in my mind homeschooling would eliminate this completely.

"With time, however, I adapted and learned that homeschooling did not mean I would miss out on the personal relationships I craved. In fact, by the time I graduated high school four years later, I had experienced more than the typical public high schooler might. Thanks to my aunt who homeschooled me, I got what I was afraid I was going to miss out on. I participated in competitive sports programs, including soccer, baseball, basketball, and volleyball. I took part in a student body that completed several community service projects, which required our members to solicit local business sponsorships as well as outreach to local government officials including the mayor of our city. I took a Toastmasters class with my peers to improve our public speaking skills. I experienced a coed Junior and Senior Formal event that included a trip downtown, evening wear, fine dining, and theater. I shared an annual camping trip with dozens of different families each summer, many of whom I am still close to more than twenty years later. These experiences, and many others, more than satisfied my need for social interaction and relationships throughout my homeschool experience.

"Of course, none of this would have been possible were it not for the dedicated parents, grandparents, aunt, uncles, guardians, mentors, and volunteers who took my upbringing upon themselves and helped to encourage and guide me through it all."

Jacob now homeschools his two children.

These eight scenarios are by no means comprehensive, but they represent a majority of the reasons parents give for thinking their children won't learn from them. With these reasons in hand, we have recommendations helpful to every scenario.

Tools to Help Children Learn from You

Find a Learning/Teaching Balance

There are two sides to every coin. As we discussed in chapter 2, children are natural learners. Be careful not to suppress their ability to learn by using methods of teaching that aren't working or that dishonor their unique learning capabilities. Instead, you can enhance their learning by presenting subjects and information in ways that are optimal for their unique brains, preferences, and personalities. Be the coach your children need and they will become coachable.

Change How You Teach

The approach you take to teaching your children can affect their willingness to learn from you. Observe *how* your children enjoy taking in information from you. Do they prefer to read it alongside you from a workbook, listen to you read it while they play with kinetic sand, or experience it out at a museum while you read exhibit placards and booklets? Explore environments and methods to find ones that help them connect with *you* the most. You might not be able to meet your children in this way all the time, but we suggest trying it for the easier subjects first. Also, research more about children's natural instinct to learn. John Holt wrote an entire book on it, *How Children Learn*. According to Holt:

> What is essential is to realize that children learn independently, not in bunches; that they learn out of interest and curiosity, not to please or appease the adults in power; and that they ought to be in control of their own learning, deciding for themselves what they want to learn and how they want to learn it. (Holt [1967] 2017, 278)

Change Your Mindset

When homeschooling, you can be a coach instead of a teacher. John Wooden, one of the most esteemed coaches in history, said, "Being a role model is the most powerful form of educating" (Wooden and Jamison 1997, 5). Sometimes, we can get so caught up in what we are supposed to teach and in being the "teacher" that we forget to be the role model or the coach. When you adopt the mindset of coach, you can lead by example to guide your children through their education journey with enthusiasm and heart.

You are an example—your children watch you closely and will sense your attitude toward learning. You can learn together with your children and demonstrate your interest in learning. Albert Bandura, a Stanford professor who specialized in educational psychology, developed the "social learning theory," which teaches that children will imitate behaviors that they observe, especially ones that hold interest to them. You get to be that model for your own children first and foremost, so model joy in learning. Whether you are learning something new for yourself, or learning alongside your children—remember that joy is contagious.

Share the Decision-Making

Homeschooling provides the flexibility to write learning goals together, allowing students to design and execute projects to accomplish those goals themselves. You can make sure the content is interesting to your own children. We're not saying skip teaching basic math if your children find it boring. We are saying maybe it can wait while your children learn something they have a strong interest in. This also gives you an opportunity to develop your mentoring role with them.

You can create a balance in curriculum by providing your children with content they are extremely interested in while also covering content that is critical to learn that they may find less interesting.

Letting Kids Decide

Emily, homeschool parent, Georgia and New England

Emily shared with me how she developed strong relationships with her three children: "I try to always keep in mind that my children are people, and need to feel at least a little in control of their lives, whether it's a four-year-old choosing to color trees purple or a fourteen-year-old deciding he would rather type than write for his homework. I include them in as many decisions that involve them as I can—they chose the paint for their bedrooms, they helped me build their desks, they created the schedule for school. I choose curriculum and core classes, they choose electives. I always try to have fun with them. Until recently, we would take a 'mini vacay' every few months. Sometimes my mom would go with us, on rare occasions dad could come too. I told them I'd drive six hours in one direction, max, so they looked at what science centers had reciprocal memberships with ours, where the cool zoos and aquariums and such were (stuff that interested them), and we did a lot of cool things on the cheap. I honestly think my kids have the relationships they do with us because we treated them with love and respect."

Outsource the Teaching, Enhance the Learning

You don't have to do all the teaching yourself. There are no rules about you having to provide all the instruction when you homeschool your children. You can find other resources for specific content or subjects, and still be there as the coach.

Online Curriculum

There is an abundance of curriculum available online. Students can log in, watch a lesson, complete a digital activity, and receive feedback. As the parent, you are permitted access to track and monitor their progress.

Video Instruction

Different from a fully online curriculum, some printed curriculum comes with video instruction for each lesson. As I mentioned previously, I found this particularly helpful when I struggled to teach basic math to my daughter. Mandi uses the same video instruction to teach herself the concepts and methods, and then she adapts it and teaches it to her daughter who wants to learn without using a screen.

In-Person Instruction

There are many options for in-person instruction for homeschoolers. There may be a co-op, enrichment center, or private teacher who offers a class for the subject(s) you want to outsource. For example, where I live, children of all ages and levels take interest-based, in-person classes from homeschool vendors, ranging from Spanish lessons and writing courses to game-making and baking.

Self-Teaching

If your child readily follows instructions and learns well on their own, let them. Children are able to understand a great deal on their own, sometimes surprisingly quickly. Homeschooling releases them to pursue learning autonomously at their own pace. Find materials, sources, or curriculum designed for students to read or listen to independently. Make a plan to check in on their progress and assess their understanding regularly.

Coaching our children through this season of life can be hard, especially when they don't want to learn from us. But take heart, our vision for our children's education is bigger than the current battle.

Can-Do Assessment to Help My Child Learn from Me

❑ I can observe my child and determine what sparks their interests and curiosity.

❑ I can figure out *why* my child "won't" learn from me using the scenarios presented in this chapter.

❑ I can identify a way I taught in the past that was ineffective and can use a different method to help my child learn from me in a new way. I can test the new way on something small and see if it works.

❑ I can offer my child choices in content, environment, or schedule that I am comfortable with in order to help them experience self-direction and autonomy.

❑ I can try a mindset shift, moving from thinking of myself in a teacher role to thinking of myself as a guide or coach.

Chapter 4

I Want to Homeschool, but What If I Don't Have the Patience?

MANDI

Let's be honest, many of us have lost our patience with our kids at some point. Whether we express it in the tone or volume of our voice or by simply acting annoyed, we regret it and wish it hadn't happened. We practice skills that improve our patience and try to avoid situations that make us vulnerable to losing it again. It's part of the refining process of parenthood. Similarly, homeschooling can be trying at times. We don't stop parenting our children just because we don't always have the patience, however, and the same goes for homeschooling.

You might be thinking, "Adding homeschooling to the list of parenting duties might be too much and cause my patience to break!" When it comes to this particular struggle, being with our children for extended hours can seem overwhelming. You are probably familiar with the stereotype of parents celebrating "back to school" season as droves of children go back to full-time classes and parents get the break they've been pining for all summer.

We challenge you to consider that it doesn't have to be that way. With a little shift of perspective, perhaps homeschooling can become an extension of parenting, where the struggles are balanced with joys and accomplishments. Rather than let your worries about your personal patience prevent you from homeschooling, consider these solutions that we hope will resonate with you and show you that you can do this.

Step 1: Know the Root Cause

Most of us struggle in various ways with patience. Homeschooling may bring this out, so it's important to know what causes our impatience so we can address it. The following reasons for losing patience when homeschooling will be addressed throughout this chapter:

- Seasons of life—There are seasons of parenthood that challenge patience more than others. Trying to homeschool older children while caring for toddlers and infants can be extremely challenging.

- Learning challenges—Perhaps you have a child with learning challenges; that can certainly cause the most composed parent to lose patience at times. We address this particular challenge in chapters 3 and 17.

- Pressing deadlines—Sometimes you want your children to learn something quickly or before you head out for a day with friends. Deadlines definitely place pressure on the parent and can cause you to impatiently try to force something to happen.

- Personal well-being—Maybe it is your own fatigue, or a lack of nutrition, exercise, or downtime that is causing you to struggle with patience. It's hard to be patient when you aren't operating at your best.

- Sensory sensitivities—Some parents struggle with their own sensory sensitivities, and it seems that children can overstimulate their senses quite quickly.

 Mistakes We Made

Jessica

Since becoming a mom, I've learned that I have sensory sensitivities exacerbated by noise and touch. Once I'm overstimulated, I become impatient and snap at my children. Unfortunately, this happens even while homeschooling. I may be reading a lesson with my eleven-year-old daughter while my five-year-old son is in my lap. It's fine until she starts tapping her pencil on the table and he starts singing quietly to himself while wiggling in my lap. Then, I lose it. I yell at my kids to stop and sit still while listening to the lesson—which is not something I even believe they need to do! I believe it is okay for my children to keep their hands or bodies busy while they are actively listening to me, but when I'm overstimulated, it's too much for me to handle. I wish I could say that knowing my triggers and taking care of myself makes everything perfect, but it doesn't. The reality is that I have to continually work on my patience, recognize my limits, and practice taking breaks every day. I apologize to my children when I lose my patience and yell. I work hard on letting my kids know when I am feeling sensitive and need a change. Letting them in helps them see that I'm not perfect but that I can advocate for what I need and they can help care for me.

Even the most patient of parents and teachers have breaking points. It is important to identify where ours are, what triggers them, and to know our limits. As Joan Erikson, the wife of developmental psychologist Erik Erikson, has observed, "The more you know yourself, the more patience you have for what you see in others" (Goleman 1988).

Step 2: Address the Root Cause

Knowing why we are short on patience, and the triggers that affect us, is only the beginning. We have to address the root in order to find solutions for managing our patience levels. Whether you decide to homeschool or not, we hope the following solutions will be helpful to you as a parent.

Learn Your Limits

If trying to homeschool during a particular season of life seems challenging, take heart: it doesn't last long. Children will grow and change, and so will the challenges we face as parents. If looming or unmet deadlines trigger impatient responses, avoid setting them and instead appreciate the amount of progress made in a book or activity. If expectations repeatedly lead to disappointment, reframe your outlook for next time, and communicate your expectations to your kids.

If you have a night when you didn't get much sleep, maybe don't try that complicated science experiment; instead redirect energy to an audiobook, games, and free play the next day. Being aware of root causes allows you to pay attention to external and internal triggers and sense when you are reaching a limit.

 Mistakes We Made

Mandi

I love to add lots of ambiance to our home learning time together. One morning we had about an hour to read poetry and study the works of Beethoven and Rembrandt. So I made strawberry scones and strawberry tea, and served it with our fine tea dishes. I was excited for our special time together as I lit a scented candle and turned on twinkle lights. My kids gathered and devoured their scones and tea, and before long, one or two kids started asking, "Can we be done?" and "It's almost time to leave. When will we be done?"

I was crestfallen and couldn't hold my disappointment in any longer as I burst into tears. "We are learning about beautiful things in life! You are lucky you got scones and tea to go with it!" And I left the room in sniffles.

What I am still learning is that I need to communicate my expectations to my children, but also not expect my children to act exactly the way I would. It is still special to have tea and scones and learn about beautiful things together, even if the participants want it to end earlier than I expected.

Make a Game Plan to Retain or Regain Your Patience

Developing and implementing a game plan helps defuse a patience-draining situation and gives you time to adjust before reaching a breaking point. You can plan alternative activities ahead of time with input from your co-parent and children.

Game Plan Ideas

Take a break for

- wiggles
- snacks
- quiet time
- free time

Go outside for

- a nature lesson
- a picnic
- bike riding/roller skating
- a walk

Prioritize Self-Care to Reset

This sounds ridiculous to many parents, because self-care can seem like a luxury that most just can't attain. What we mean by "self-care" is finding ways to reset your mind to be less easily triggered. Establishing a unique set of rituals will help you be at your best. Self-care might include:

- meditation
- prayer
- reading
- exercise
- time spent on a hobby
- time alone

Not every rejuvenating ritual can be done while the kids are in your sole care, so find ways to prioritize *you* a little bit each day. Jessica listens to audiobooks while doing dishes or taking an evening shower. Mandi loves to listen to Bob Marley or read books on parenting.

A Note on Mental Health

If you feel like the stress or pressure of homeschooling could trigger existing or preexisting mental health struggles, you may want to talk with a mental health professional before embarking on this lifestyle change. Consider your support group and ask co-parents, grandparents, and supportive friends to share the educational load or household work during the transition. Take your time and lay the groundwork of developing routines, rhythms, and habits that can help stabilize the family prior to starting your first day of homeschooling. In the end, if you do not feel up to the task of homeschooling, it's okay! You need to do what is best for you and your family.

Focus on Relationships

With homeschooling, we have time to prioritize our relationships with our children over our goals to accomplish tasks. And we get to do this while they are learning. This shift in priority may help with our children's willingness to learn from us. For example, instead of trying to cram in a lesson on tying shoelaces before you run out the door, you can find a time to focus on this skill at a relaxed pace, with plenty of encouragement and fun.

In addition, we get to fix mistakes that we made in exasperation. We can balance negative interactions with positive ones. Consider John Gottman's "magic relationship ratio" (Benson, n.d.). Intended for marriages, this 5:1 ratio may also be a helpful tool for nourishing our parent-child relationships. For each negative interaction, we need five positive ones. If we speak hurtful words out of frustration, we can balance that with a sincere apology, intentional affection, interest in our child's activities, and so on. Being together most of the day allows the connection we have with our children to be one of positivity and harmony, instead of one of dissonance and discord.

Find Support

To be the best homeschool parents we can be, we need to prioritize our mental health. This means we need a support system we can rely on. These people may offer words of encouragement, empathy, validation, and helpful suggestions; they may even offer physical support such as child care. We can find support beyond family and friends through social media, faith-based communities, neighbors, and other homeschoolers—the homeschool community can be a fantastic support.

Outsource

We've mentioned this before and it's worth saying again—others can help. You do not need to go this journey alone. Finding the physical and mental help you need can aid in sustaining your patience.

- Classes—Enrichment centers, online learning, co-ops, and extracurriculars break up the day when needed, offering you a reprieve while keeping your children engaged and learning.
- Visits with others—Schedule a video call or hang-out time during the day to allow family and friends the opportunity to connect with your child.

Invest Time in a Community

Growing in community (chapter 9), particularly with homeschooling families who understand our unique struggles, provides camaraderie, understanding, and support for good days and bad days as a homeschool parent. Knowing we are not alone is powerful and can provide strength when we need it most.

Plan Accordingly

Think about your needs, your goals for homeschooling, and the support system you can employ to make it all work. Planning ahead for breaks is incredibly helpful to avoid burnout and fatigue. Homeschoolers have a unique flexibility to customize educational hours to best suit their individual families—use this to your advantage.

In summary, yes, you will at times lose your patience while homeschooling your children. But there are many ways to manage this. We think the net benefits of homeschooling are well worth the hard work to overcome impatience.

Can-Do Assessment to Help Me with My Patience

❏ I can identify what triggers my impatience.

❏ I can make a list of effective self-care tools and find moments in my day to focus on one or two of these.

❏ I can make a game plan to find a mental balance that will help me maintain patience in parenting and homeschooling.

❏ I can find a support network to rely on to give me the breaks necessary to be my best.

❏ I can find opportunities to outsource a portion of my child's time each week to allow me a break.

Chapter 5

I Want to Homeschool, but What If I Don't Have the Space?

MANDI

No space? No problem! Homeschooling doesn't require much space, and it certainly doesn't take a classroom to educate children. Some families trade out a guest bedroom, convert a family room, or finish their garage to create a classroom, but none of that is necessary for providing a quality education. With some minimal organization and a few seating options, learning can happen anywhere, inside and outside the home. Freedom to experience learning anywhere is a beautiful homeschool advantage. The world is our classroom.

Learning Inside the Home

Every room is a learning place, whether or not we hang a whiteboard or border the walls with the alphabet. Every room provides an opportunity to create enriching experiences, and it does not need to—nor should it—look like a classroom. This shift in mindset might take some time for you and your child to make, but it is necessary for creating a learning space and experience unique to your family. (This is part of the process we referred to in chapter 3 and our Quick Start Guide, known as "deschooling.")

Kyle D. Pruett, clinical professor of child psychiatry at Yale School of Medicine, explains that nonschool settings such as museums and libraries highly support playful learning, which encourages the growth of a child's executive function, also known as self-control and self-awareness (Pruett 2019). Instead of modeling our home learning spaces after a classroom, we can think of libraries with large open spaces to pursue one's curiosity. Many libraries have already figured out how to create enriching learning environments for free play and exploration (Gray, Solomon, and Tatgenhorst 2022).

At the Kitchen Table or Countertop

Homeschooling around a table allows my children to engage each other socially, emotionally, and academically while sharing their independent and collaborative creations with one another, whether art projects, storytelling, or games. When I am needed for instruction, I use a small, handheld whiteboard at the table with my children. A kitchen table is also a smart option for art projects, crafts, or tactile activities, allowing you to easily reach and help children when needed.

On the Floor

Since the moment my children were born, the floor has been a regular destination for all types of exploratory play. No matter the age, the floor can still be the most comfortable spot to learn and create, nestled in a pile of pillows on a shag rug or a beanbag chair. When you are part of the learning, you can grab your teacher's guide, your children's clipboards or workbooks, and a few pencils, and you are ready to engage as well.

On the Bed

Children can learn lying down. Literally! Whether you are playing card games together or creating a comic book, your bed or theirs can be a comfy, cuddly oasis. For one entire year, my bed was a quiet sanctuary where my children learned math, using their student workbooks and the instructor's DVD.

In Your Child's Room

A small desk, the floor, and the bed with a cutting board borrowed from the kitchen to use as a firm surface are all suitable for learning in your child's room. Their books and supplies can be kept on a shelf or in drawers for easy access.

To capitalize on my daughter's immense interest in storytelling, one night I gifted her an activity book on writing strategies. The next morning, she proudly showed me her progress in the book. She learned a remarkable amount in one night because she was highly receptive in that space and at that time.

In Your Yard, or on Your Patio or Balcony

If you can fit a couple of chairs outside or add some fake turf or an outdoor mat to lie on, you have an entirely new learning space with a different perspective and some fresh air. A balcony or rooftop garden can be a beautiful spot for children to peacefully view the world while creating and designing their next escape room adventure. Bouncing on a trampoline or juggling a soccer ball also provides a healthy activity while listening to read-alouds of *Charlotte's Web*, The Chronicles of Narnia, or The Penderwicks series.

No matter where you go in your home, it can be a learning space. You can provide options allowing for self-direction, creativity, and exploration to help your children find what works best for them. Research shows that student choice and informed decision-making deeply affect brain development, so allow choice whenever you can (Stixrud and Johnson 2019). Try it and see if it works.

Learning Outside the Home

A well-rounded education is founded on a variety of experiences. Whether you are in the car, on a hike, or exploring at a zoo, learning outside the home can be a ray of sunshine in your child's life. As research shows, an important part of an enriched education is experiential learning (Kolb 2015). One multisensory lesson can be learning to read maps while walking to a local park, with the scent of springtime blossoms in the air and the touch of the wind on your faces. Try attending or participating in an entrepreneurial fair, forming a tutoring club for at-risk youth, or taking an art class together at a local community college. Just being out in the world can motivate a child to learn more about it.

In the Car

Experiencing life together sometimes requires a bit of driving time. You get to choose how to use this time. Going places in the car can provide:

- your children's undivided attention for important conversations and meaningful discussions on their studies
- a quiet space in the day for parents or children to meditate on life or reflect on learning experiences
- an atmosphere of active listening for read-aloud stories, second language practice, music appreciation, and memorization

Sometimes the best part of the day is when we are heading somewhere together.

On Public Transit

Public transit can be a memorable place to engage your children. Your hands are available to snuggle your little one, practice math problems together, edit your child's essay, teach street smarts, and make observations about the world flying by outside your window. My son and I discussed *Murder on the Orient Express* for our Mother-Son Book Club while riding the local commuter train. We bumped into the train engineer on his shift change and conducted an impromptu interview, learning about the educational and career path for train engineers. Besides being an efficient use of time, public transit offers opportunities for children to gain awareness of their environment and learn life skills, which include:

- learning about maps, legends, cardinal directions, and transfer options for navigating a city transit system
- practicing buying bus and train tickets using kiosks or an app
- adopting appropriate behavior and social rules when boarding, riding, and engaging other passengers
- exposure to city and country sights that can only be seen from a train's window

- gaining contextual knowledge for content they are learning in books and textbooks
- riding with friends and getting to enjoy learning opportunities together

At a Destination

Besides experiential learning, outside the home can be a great place for bookwork. We have hiked to beautiful views to learn math, regularly read aloud while our children swung on trees, and watched chimpanzees at the zoo groom their armpits while studying animal books. You can customize homeschool spaces based on your children's interests. Sit in a reading nook at a bookstore or library, or simply bring the day's bookwork and activities to a grandparent's home, a coffee shop, or bakery. With a bag of snacks and schoolbooks, we have accomplished full school days while waiting in lines at Disneyland, sitting on a blanket at the beach watching the sea lions, or having a picnic on a park bench. Learning can truly happen anywhere, even when it's bookwork.

School Where You Need To

Naomi, homeschool parent, single, working full time

We met Naomi, who has a two-year-old and homeschools her eight-year-old son. She shared: "I am a single mom (one income, no child support) and I work full time, forty hours per week. [My son] gets all his schoolwork done at the Boys and Girls Club in my office building before the kids get there in the afternoon. I have a coworker who also brings her homeschooled kids there early, so my son will take breaks and play with them. I know I have a very unique situation where I am allowed to bring my son to work with me all day, and this is the number one thing that has allowed me to homeschool. Taking him to the Boys and Girls Club allows him to see his friends every day and also do all the hands-on STEM activities and messy art activities that I don't have time to do at home!"

Storage

It is necessary to have at least a small collection of books, enriching materials, and creative tools at your child's fingertips, and these items need space. These ideas for space saving can help:

- Use baskets and store them in empty spaces like room corners or atop shelves.

- Spend regular time at the library for access to an unlimited book supply, craft experiences, and literature-based events; borrow and return to cut down on storage needs.

- Use storage bins in closets, under beds, and in the garage for book rotation.

- Consider unwanted completed workbooks worthy of the recycle bin.

- Schedule a regular purge day each semester, and take pictures or save digital versions of work you want to keep.

- Donate used books to libraries or used bookstores (which sometimes give store credit!).

- Purchase an inexpensive utility cart to store curriculum, art supplies, printer paper, and educational tools and games.

Tiny Home Homeschooling

Jessica, homeschool parent of two children, ages five and eleven

At the beginning of my homeschool journey, we were living in a tiny home of just 700 square feet. Storage space was tight, but I got creative with the space we had. I opted for a smaller dining table which doubled as our school table. This left space to line a wall with storage cubes for books, art supplies, puzzles, games, and more. My super-handy mom built two twin bed frames with hinging tops to serve as our couches and storage. I used the wall in my hallway to mount a learning clock, a latch board, and a large oil drip pan to use for magnetic letters and numbers. It was a sweet time of life for us to homeschool together in our little space with our little kids.

When I catch a glimpse of my kids writing stories under their sheets with a flashlight or even reading in the bathroom, my heart fills with joy. "Do you want to make a fort with our kitchen table or on the trampoline while we learn about nomads?" "How about we practice our math with chalk on the sidewalk?" "Let's try shouting the eight parts of speech on a park swing as we soar in the air." We can define what homeschooling looks and feels like for our own families, inside and outside our homes. We don't need lots of space; we need the freedom of choice and the creativity that comes with making our unique space work for us. Our homeschooling can happen anywhere.

Can-Do Assessment to Identify Spaces for Homeschooling

- ☐ I can use a table, counter, or cutting board in my home for creating a learning space during the day.
- ☐ I can make space on the floor or bed into a comfortable place to learn.
- ☐ I am able to transport learning materials with us to learn in places outside our home.
- ☐ I can think of fun or peaceful places in my community where we can complete bookwork.
- ☐ I have unused spaces or room corners that can hold baskets or a small utility cart.

Chapter 6

I Want to Homeschool, but What If I Don't Know What to Do All Day?

MANDI

What do we do all day? Whatever we want!

Being together during summer (a mere ten to twelve weeks) is one thing, but perpetual, unending time with your children is entirely different and can be quite intimidating for some. We see how this causes hesitation, so this chapter addresses the five main essentials of a homeschool day: academics, free time, intentional time together, outsourced learning, and friendship time. Plus, we provide a few ways we and others structure the homeschool day.

It is a common misconception that a homeschool day is all about academics. It is not. It is about these five essentials. While academics can be the foundation for many future careers, providing a balanced education ensures your children are progressing toward becoming who they want to be. Let us all live with purpose and enjoy living life to its fullest. We share our perspective on the five essentials so you can imagine what your day could look like if you decide to choose this lifestyle. (We do not actually experience all five essentials on a daily basis, though we try to be intentional throughout the week, fitting them in when it makes the most sense in our routines and rhythms.)

Homeschooling Terms

Here we provide definitions for terms in the context of homeschooling (see the glossary for additional definitions). It's important to note that in homeschooling, defining terms is not always crystal clear; definitions vary based upon the philosophy and lens of the homeschool parents.

academics—subjects that require studying and reasoning useful for philosophical ideas, debate, and knowledge; typically includes math, language arts, history, and science. Academics can be taught through textbooks, workbooks, and other methods that people often associate with school, but they can also be taught through cooking, travel, life experiences, and more.

education—the *process* of taking in and storing information in our brains to enlighten and form our foundational perspectives, values, ethics, skills, and relationships. Education can be delivered formally through direct instruction or guidance—with books, games, experiences, field trips, technology, and teamwork—or informally through experiencing life's daily challenges, travel, reading, and relationships.

learning—the knowledge or skill *acquired* through a lesson or informative process.

teaching—the *sharing* of knowledge, skills, or experiences through teacher-centered (what the teacher decides to teach) or student-centered (what the student chooses to learn) means.

Essential #1: Academics

For us, the importance of academics for homeschooling stems from a belief in teaching subjects with a "life lens." *Life lens* is a term we use to help us view academics as a forward look at our children's entire lives instead of focusing only on the here and now. Tailoring our mindset to this lens is one of the major benefits of homeschooling.

The Life Lens

Consider the lens *you* use to look at academics. If your focus is on worksheets, tests, and grades, you may need to shift your lens to focus on learning for learning's sake. Some examples include the following:

- We learn to read so we can soak in beautiful literature, learn helpful information for life skills, develop empathy, and enjoy creative storytelling.
- We learn math to be able to manage our money well and solve real-life problems.
- We learn science so we can explore natural laws that allow us to dwell in wonder about the beauty of life all around us.
- We learn history so we can make wise decisions, be responsible citizens, learn compassion for those different from ourselves, and find perspective.
- We learn languages so we can communicate within and outside our communities and make a difference in people's lives directly.
- We learn art and music to experience them more deeply, express ourselves with nonverbal communication, and gift others with our own expressions.
- We learn economics and environmental science so we can serve our family, community, and others outside of our community with heartfelt joy and gladness.

Even when you choose to homeschool with this life lens, you might find curriculum, college applications, and career requirements divert your gaze back to testing, grades, and transcripts. It's easy for many homeschoolers to lose sight of the life lens. If you commit to this new lens, though, as your paradigm shifts, you will start to notice that you might test less and discuss more. Instead of loads of worksheets, your days may be filled with wonder, discussion, practice, and purpose.

How Long and How Often

The amount of time required for homeschooling varies depending on state laws. However, an even broader spectrum of variance depends on the family. Each family's home school looks different since it depends on schedule, curriculum, educational approach, challenges, and the ages of the children. In my home, often, the academic portion of a homeschool day with my middle- and elementary-level children is about one to three hours. The rest of our educational time is spent exploring and learning in other ways. Jessica's eleven-year-old nephew, Paxton, shared that his favorite thing about homeschooling is that his school day doesn't take as long to complete as that of his neighborhood friends who are at a traditional school. He says, "The longest I have ever spent on my schoolwork in one day is four hours."

I concentrate on academics during the typical nine-month school year, while our summer learning is focused on robotics, piano, Spanish, and character development. Some parents, like Jessica, teach academics during the summer too. She takes a year-round approach to homeschooling and continues academics at a relaxed pace through the summer.

Different subjects require different frequencies of study, so we don't always devote time to every subject every day. One of the glories of the homeschool lifestyle is that we get to choose. Over the years I have witnessed that my children lose their math skills if they do not practice them almost daily. So, I incorporate math into our daily routine. However, in our family, we do not learn history every day—but sometimes history is the entirety of our day. Because my children were fascinated by the musical *Hamilton*, one entire school day consisted of reading aloud *Who Was Alexander Hamilton?*, discussing his role in United States history, watching videos about him, and capping off the day by enjoying *Hamilton* the musical.

A Bit of Balance

Marie, homeschool parent of a tween and a teen

Marie shares how she balances the time spent on various subjects and curriculum to adapt to her children's abilities: "One of my kids flies through all of his language arts subjects completely independently, but then slows to a stop with math. I sit with him, and we take our time. We go at his pace, and we don't move on until he feels like he has understood the topic. My other kid can do almost all of his math problems mentally and soars through them, but he finds some of his language arts lessons totally boring. So, I work with him on that to keep him engaged. Also, when it comes to curriculum, if it is a topic that my kids master with ease, we can skip the review work and get to the next new topic."

Essential #2: Free Time

Everyone needs free time—including you. We make sure our children have plenty of time to work and play autonomously. We resist the urge to insert ourselves, and instead we try to be available for our children to invite us to join in or help them. We are still involved in this part of our children's day—we just aren't in charge of it. Allowing children to dictate their own rules builds their ability to self-regulate, helps them learn decision-making, and helps develop their sense of self-control. The best part is that this autonomy develops internal motivation (Stixrud and Johnson 2019). A big gift of homeschooling is that we don't have to limit free time; we can give hours to it.

Screen Time Limits

Parents and professionals sometimes disagree with each other and within their own circles about the amount of screen time that should be allowed for children and their developing brains. Within homeschool communities there is also much debate about restrictions and autonomy regarding screens during free time. In my home, we have established limits based upon our wisdom as parents and the recommendations of experts we choose to listen to. Computers, tablets, and other types of screens can offer wonderful ways to learn lessons, research topics, practice problem-solving, and take classes from experts or professionals in a field of interest. They also allow our children to try programming, and create digital art and writing projects. At the same time, we highly value time spent in activities away from screens and encourage such activities during free time.

Pursuing Interests

During free time, our children pursue activities such as these:

- designing informational books
- researching animal facts
- planting fruit seeds in a jar
- practicing wall ball
- coding video games
- memorizing scripts
- reading graphic novels
- dancing to made-up songs
- writing guitar sheet music
- trying a new cookie recipe

- dreaming up new board games

- building a bike ramp

- starting a pen pal club

- experimenting with movie-making software

Free time allows our children space in their day to pursue whatever piques their interests.

Individualized Special Time

As a side benefit for larger families, while one child works or plays independently, we can make time to guide the other children separately, since their needs might be different. Planning for a long block of free time allows us plenty of time to spend with each child in turn.

Notable Homeschooler

Christopher Paolini, author of the *New York Times* bestselling book *Eragon*, was homeschooled his entire academic career. He credits his parents, particularly his mother, for making his dream of publishing a book a reality because of their homeschooling lifestyle. He learned at an accelerated pace so he could finish high school by the age of fifteen, and then focus on writing *Eragon* before beginning college. He says, "Homeschooling gave me the opportunity to pursue my own interests, time to dream, and time to write. And I had freedoms the majority of today's teens don't have" (Paolini 2015).

While living in Montana, he had the freedom and time to build a forge so he could make knives and swords. He also learned to spin wool, build survival shelters, fell trees, and track wild game to build his background knowledge in preparation for writing.

The Gift of Boredom

That's right. Boredom is a gift to our children. When given free time, our children have to figure out how to spend their time in a satisfying way. Whether it's diving into a pile of books, setting up an imaginary store, digging for worms outside, or building a city out of toy bricks, boredom can be the catalyst for creative thinking. My husband wrote an award-winning poem when he was twelve years old because, as he says, "I was bored."

Free time offers many benefits for the homeschooler. Making choices throughout one's day and taking ownership over one's own learning can be empowering and fun. Observing how our children play educates us in how our children learn. A child may be more of a hands-on learner, or they may be more interested in stories. Free time will help us observe that. Then, we will be able to curate the other essentials for them.

Essential #3: Intentional Time Together

It's crucial to provide time in our day for a combination of games, important conversations, body movement, and memory-making experiences. If we are too structured and narrow in planning, we won't have the space for an essential part of a homeschool day—intentional time together. We make the space for organic parenting and spontaneous learning through these things:

- Games and experiments—Research shows that using traditional games to learn science and social studies can improve elementary-age children's "creative thinking skills" in comparison with conventional learning (Arga, Nurfurqon, and Nurani 2020).

- Conversations—Important topics and life lessons naturally arise throughout the day, so utilize those moments to talk about the practical, meaningful, and tough things in life.

- Movement—You can create an obstacle course, try a push-up challenge in between subjects, go on a bike ride or walk, or try a brain warm-up video. The important thing is that the movement is done together.

- Experiences—Explore museums, gardens, zoos, parks, and more. Experiences can be a memorable homeschool treat for the whole family. While studying Japan, my family spent two hours at the local Japanese Friendship Gardens, ate Japanese candy, learned about koi fish, and read aloud Japanese legends.

- Theme days—You can pick a date and plan a day around a theme that interests your child. You can plan it on your own or together with your child. My children were obsessed with Jeff Kinney's Diary of a Wimpy Kid series. When they finished the entire series, I planned a theme day to celebrate with book-related experiments and games, an author biography read-aloud, and time laughing together as we read aloud our favorite *Calvin and Hobbes* stories (one of Kinney's favorite reads).

- Morning time—Consider gifting yourself and your kids time together each morning to sit and reflect on the world's beauty. Whether you each share a gratitude, study van Gogh's *The Starry Night*, tune your ear to a piece by Mozart, or read a poem from Shel Silverstein's collection, you know you started the day off with something that touches the heart.

Essential #4: Outsourced Learning

Many homeschoolers set aside part of their days for outsourced learning opportunities that are based on the needs and interests of their children.

Lessons and Sports

Whether it's ukulele, ballet, or soccer, lessons and sports leagues are a formal way our children get to pursue interests and passions. Let's be explorers of our children's interests.

Does your child love doodling? Gift your child art lessons. Does your child tap a beat at the kitchen table? Arrange for music lessons—in person, online, or perhaps by bartering with an experienced musical neighbor or friend. Figuring out if an interest is purely situational or truly an individual passion becomes clear as you continue the exposure. These types of enrichment activities might become a major building block for your child's future career or a lifetime hobby.

If it brings your child deep enjoyment, spend more time on it. If not, and there is no commitment, then let it go.

Courses, Enrichment Schools, and Theater Arts Provided by Others

There are numerous educational organizations that provide courses in person and online for homeschooled students. Outsourcing academic subjects (e.g., science labs or robotics), enrichment centers (e.g., farm schools and art schools), and theater arts can greatly enhance your child's homeschool day. Hybrid homeschool charter and private schools (available in many states) may offer two-day-a-week programs, leaving you with three days at home with your child. Even some amusement parks offer weekly educational classes to homeschooled children and teens.

If you live in an area without many options, Outschool (outschool.com) is a nationwide online marketplace with a variety of courses for various ages and interests. Outsourced courses and enrichment schools can range from an hour to an all-day experience. With some time spent in research or making community connections, you can find outsourcing options locally and online.

Mentored Learning

Grandparents, older siblings, extended family members, friends, and others have a different world of knowledge and expertise that can offer valuable learning experiences to our children. In times past, adolescents would apprentice to learn a skill or trade. By homeschooling, we can provide our children with exposure to some of these skills and trades on a smaller scale when we bring in an expert.

My engineer dad built a mini-Disneyland in his backyard (with a little help from my kids) and helped my daughter design a ride: Ruby's Safari. All my children worked on the art, plastered and painted objects, and designed the ride mechanisms.

Does your family or circle of friends include any writers, carpenters, graphic designers, or gardening experts? When we homeschool, we can tap into this wealth of knowledge and expertise with mentorship as an integral part of our homeschool week.

Essential #5: Friendship Time

The other four essentials provide opportunities for socializing with siblings or friends during activities and allow for plenty of fun, friendship navigation, and self-regulation practice. For highly social children, an additional play date or hangout may be needed daily, weekly, or monthly—it depends on the situation and child.

Our co-op meets a few times a month for an adventure, learning experience, or book club discussion (see chapter 9 for more about co-ops). With other friends, we have a weekly hangout. Sometimes the hangout is the entire homeschool day depending on the adventure, lesson, or activity. We gauge the needs of our own children and determine how to meet them.

Ways to Customize Your Homeschool Day

Now that we've reviewed our five main essentials of homeschooling, we want to share how you can customize them for yourself. This is what makes homeschooling a unique journey for each family.

Write a Mission Statement

One of the best things about homeschooling is that it's arranged around your family and the educational lifestyle you want. Some homeschoolers write a mission statement with reasons for why they homeschool, infusing it with intention and hope. They use the mission statement to gauge their decisions. They plan their routines and schedules in a manner that will support the reasons why they homeschool. They consider goals, tactics, and time line, and pick strategies they can control.

Part of my family's mission statement is to make memories and grow our connections through fun and challenging experiences together. To ensure we don't experience mission drift, I pick specific curriculum, group experiences, family time, and adventures to meet our mission.

Before deciding to homeschool, ask yourself and your kids to answer questions like the following:

- What will make my week or month great?

- How can I grow this week?

- What is one way we can challenge each other to grow this month?

- What interests should we pursue this week or month?

- Name one favorite activity to do or goal to work toward this week.

While these questions aid in writing a homeschool mission statement, more importantly, they may help you answer the ultimate question of whether or not to homeschool. Many find that the intentionality of the homeschool lifestyle helps them more easily bring their family's mission to life.

A Pandemic Consideration

Mai and Nguyen, homeschool parents of three elementary-age children, California

Mai and Nguyen were thrown into schooling at home when the COVID-19 pandemic sent everyone home for virtual schooling. After the school year ended, they committed to homeschooling through a public charter school's independent study program. This new lifestyle was something they had never considered before the pandemic. One of the first aspects Mai noticed was the schedule flexibility that homeschooling allowed. "I appreciated the freedom and autonomy aspect. That's a reason why we chose to homeschool, to not follow a rigorous and rigid schedule."

Consider Personalities in Your Daily Scheduling

Consider yourself and your children. Your personalities and preferences can dictate how you organize the five essentials in your days and weeks. If any of you thrive on schedules, make a schedule. If you thrive on routines, make a routine. Then, if you don't get to the last item on your list, you can start the next day with that item and continue on with the routine. Consistency and structure can be grounding for children and can give them a sense of control over their environment. Free time and intentional time together can rule your day if you don't want schedules or routines.

Examples of Homeschool Schedules

Every family organizes their day differently. There are many options for schedules. In the next section, we provide a few sample schedules to demonstrate the flexibility and freedom to design the home life that is best for you. At the end of the chapter, we share details of a single day in the life of a homeschool family.

We want to point out that the entire day is educational, incorporating the various essentials of homeschooling. Since homeschoolers consider homeschooling a lifestyle of education and connection, we have included schedules from waking to sleeping to show that learning doesn't stop in the evening. Sometimes children are most open to learning and growing during their peaceful nightly bedtime routine, with journaling, reading, and listening to historical stories. An educational lifestyle can be bookended with sleep.

The "Daily Routine" Schedule

If you or your children thrive on routine, then a daily schedule might be a good fit.

Monday through Thursday	
Time	**Activity**
8–10 a.m.	Wake-up, free time
10 a.m.–noon	Academics (math, science, history, language arts, etc.)
after lunch	Co-op meetups, classes, art, hands-on science, or other activities
dinner–bedtime	Family time, games, table talk, free time, bedtime routine

Fridays are for enjoying nature, such as hiking with the co-op.

The "Every Day Is Different" Schedule

This is an example of a homeschool week for my family when my children were ages nine, eleven, and thirteen. While each day may be different, a daily checklist for independent work including gratitude, the math assignment, music practice, and chores, provided some regularity. In our family, it's up to our children to learn to manage their time so they finish their daily checklist in a manner that works with their unique schedules. This exercise teaches our children personal responsibility and time management. In addition to their checklist, our children participated in learning activities throughout the week led by various educators, primarily me.

Day	Activity
Monday	Three blocks of time, about 1–2 hours each, starting after breakfast. Blocks include academics (history, science, language arts, math guidance), free time, intentional time together, etc. Free time is typically available after work is completed during each block of time, or for a few hours before sports activities. Sports are in the early evening, and read-alouds are in the evening and in bed at night. Monday is also a potential field trip day.
Tuesday	Robotics club 9 a.m.–1 p.m.; athletic cross-training with friends 2–3 p.m.; piano lessons 3:30–4:30 p.m.; and roller skating with friends 5–7 p.m. Audiobooks and Spanish practice in the car. If we don't go to piano lessons and roller skating (seasonal), then my spouse teaches a Latin lesson and reads aloud, or we have an evening of free time before bedtime.
Wednesday	Monthly co-op 10 a.m.–1 p.m. Afternoons are for field trips, playdates, sports, games, academics, or free time at home. Repeat Monday schedule on non-co-op Wednesdays. Youth group activities 6–8 p.m.
Thursday	Free time in the morning; writing class 10–11:30 a.m.; lunch playdate 11:30 a.m.–12:30 p.m.; athletic cross-training 1–2 p.m.; gymnastics class 2:30–3:30 p.m.; golf lesson; grocery shopping in the evening on the way home; free time and read aloud before bedtime

Friday	Same as Mondays, or field trips, co-op adventures, and spending time with grandparents.
Weekend	Family and friend time, educational and sports activities, games, read-alouds, and more.

The "Parent Working Part-Time" Schedule (Using Block Scheduling)

Time	Activity
7–8 a.m.	Morning routines—parent prepares for the day, exercises, and meditates; children play or prepare for the day
8:30–9 a.m.	Morning time—begin with beauty (poetry, art, music, gratitude, etc.); this can include breakfast too
9 a.m.–noon	Group and individual learning (history, science, math, writing, reading, areas of interest)
noon–1 p.m.	Lunch—shared time for a read-aloud, craft, game, etc.
1–1:30 p.m.	Close the day—connect with fun activity and prepare for the next day
1:30–5:30 p.m.	Work for the parent; free time/outsourced learning and sports for the kids (utilizing familial support if needed)
5:30–8 p.m.	Dinner, activities (sports, lessons, etc.), chores, family time
8–10 p.m.	Bedtime for younger children; free time for teens to pursue interests, complete independent work, and talk with friends

Keep in mind that the entire day is education. Life is education. You do not need to have a start and stop time to educate; you can just live life while enjoying learning together. That's it! You get to decide what you do and when you do it. It's the ultimate freedom.

A Day in the Life of a Homeschool Family

Jessica, parent of two children, ages five and eleven

On a typical Monday, I usually get out of bed at 7 a.m., starting my day by listening to the Bible while I stretch and get ready. My five-year-old son is up shortly after me, usually around 7:30 a.m. He comes to find me and without fail exclaims, "Mommy!" and jumps into my arms for the best hug. Then he immediately asks for breakfast, which is usually cereal, while I make myself coffee in the kitchen. My husband is often up by this time as well, making his way to our office where he works from home. After my son eats, we move to our dining/school room to work on something of his choice. He often chooses math and spends about twenty minutes using manipulatives to solve problems from his workbook. Then, we work on spelling for ten minutes and practice his music class lesson for fifteen minutes.

My eleven-year-old daughter wakes up around 8:30 a.m. while my son and I are still at the table. If my husband is not on a video meeting or phone call, my daughter goes straight to the piano to practice before she grabs her own breakfast. My husband and I love listening to her play, practice, and master new songs. My husband especially loves listening to her play songs from *The Lord of the Rings*. I then let my daughter choose to begin math on her own or study our history lesson together.

History is a lesson that I read aloud to both kids while my daughter completes her history workbook and my son colors in his. Sometimes, there is a related video or historical movie that we snuggle up together on the couch to watch. For math, my daughter watches a five-minute lesson from a DVD, then spends about twenty minutes completing a few pages in her math workbook. While my daughter does math, my son typically requests that I print coloring pages for him of his current favorite animal. We keep our printer next to our dining table to make it easy to access for requests like this. After my daughter is done with math and I've checked her work for understanding, we listen to our audiobook while my son continues to color. My daughter chooses something to keep her hands busy, alternating between her own coloring, tracing, or embroidery.

Lunch is usually a serve-yourself situation, so my kids each pick what they want and prepare what they are able to on their own. My husband often takes lunch at the same time, giving us a chance to all have a meal at the table together. After cleaning up lunch, my kids have the next hour for free time while I complete the laundry and dishes.

At 12:30 p.m., we hop in the car to drive to my daughter's Latin class with our co-op friends at a local coffee shop, where I talk with the moms and my son plays with the other siblings too young for the Latin class. We arrive home after Latin around 2:30 p.m. to have snacks, do some chores together, and have free time. By 3:30 p.m., my daughter and I leave for the dance studio where I teach dance classes for three hours while she dances for two and a half hours. Dancing is one of my daughter's strongest passions, so she chooses to spend her evening time this way. She also gets to be with some of her closest friends there who share the same passion. As we dance, my son has a little screen time while my husband finishes up his workday. Then my husband and son have special time to play, wrestle, watch sports, and make dinner together. My daughter and I get home at 7:30 p.m. to eat the meal my husband has waiting for us. My husband and I have a collaborative partnership that we've worked hard for and navigated together to find the right fit for our family responsibilities.

We begin the bedtime routine for my son and my daughter shortly after dinner. With both kids in bed by 9 p.m. sleeping or reading quietly, my husband and I sometimes do our own thing—me working on the computer and him playing a computer game—or we will sit down and watch a show together until we go to bed around 10:30 p.m. I spend a little time in bed reviewing my calendar and mentally preparing for the next day before falling asleep.

Can-Do Assessment to Plan My Homeschool Day

- ❏ If I decide to homeschool, I will have space in my day to allow for free time.
- ❏ I have access to board games.
- ❏ I feel comfortable reading aloud to my child, using picture books and chapter books.
- ❏ I have a person in my life with a particular skill matching my child's interest who I can ask to give of their time to mentor my child.
- ❏ I feel comfortable researching companies and organizations online or among friends for lessons and leagues of interest.
- ❏ I can provide kits, activities, crafts, or special books for my child to explore.
- ❏ I can find time during the month to meet up with others to grow friendships for my child and myself.
- ❏ I know at least one homeschool family I can meet with for support and friendship.

Chapter 7

I Want to Homeschool, but What If I Can't Afford It?

MANDI

Field trips, curriculum, and enrichment, oh my! Yes, homeschooling *can* be expensive, but it does not have to be. With a few free resources, some strategic thinking, and a willingness to tackle a challenge, you can afford to homeschool.

According to the National Home Education Research Institute (NHERI), homeschool families spend on average $600 annually per student on education (NHERI 2023). Other sources give an estimated range of $500–$1,500 per student to cover the costs of curriculum, technology, and school supplies (Lake 2022). If we stick with the $600, that is $50 per month over 12 months, or $66 per month for the typical nine-month school year. To us, that doesn't seem overly burdensome when it comes to education; however, we have more ideas to help you save money.

Free Resources for Homeschooling

An abundance of free materials and supplies is available to us; we just need to be resourceful.

- Many websites offer free educational materials for various topics and grade levels.
- Social media groups focused solely on finding and sharing free resources are available for homeschoolers to join.

- Some co-ops or homeschool groups hold an annual end-of-year exchange day where used curriculum and books can be perused and traded.

- Find a teacher your kids enjoy online—like Operation Ouch, Mr. DeMaio, and Mark Rober—for free educational content.

- Your local public park is a free and beautiful place to explore and experience nature.

- Don't overlook the library! My family's favorite history curriculum, *Story of the World*, can be checked out at our local library. Besides books, many libraries offer on-site computers and Wi-Fi, a myriad of free classes (art, life skills, etc.), and clubs. Some libraries offer laptops and hot spots to check out for an extended period of time.

- If you have an app-supporting device or computer, public library systems also have digital libraries that allow you to check out ebooks and audiobooks. You can often apply for a library card for digital items through the library's app or website, making an actual trip to the library unnecessary.

Entire days can be filled with exploration of websites (see the Free Educational Websites list below) in combination with reading library books and having discussions together.

Free Educational Websites

Education.com

HowStuffWorks

Khan Academy

Library of Congress (read.gov/kids)

Mystery Science

NASA Space Place

National Geographic Kids

The Old Farmer's Almanac

OER Commons

PBS LearningMedia

Science Bob

Smithsonian

Ted Talks for Kids

Budget-Friendly Curriculum

Explore thrift stores for books and curriculum sold at a fraction of the original price. Used-curriculum sales are popular in person and online. Web-based marketplaces offer low-cost curriculum too. I bought a "like new" cursive writing curriculum online for $15, which was less than half the price of a new package.

Prudent selection of publishers also aids in finding the right fit for children without breaking the bank. Some publishers write and organize their curriculum so that it can be bought just once for all K–12 levels. I use a reading curriculum for K–12 that was a one-time purchase of $105, and now I annually purchase only a $12 learning log for each of my children. Publishers with homeschooling curriculum lines are aware that costs need to be kept low, so many of them make curriculum available in small chunks. When we are really excited about a particular curriculum that busts our budget, we find balance by using free or budget-friendly curriculum for other subjects.

Low-Cost Enrichment and Experiences

Field trips can be a big part of a fulfilling homeschool life. Budget-conscious homeschoolers can be strategic by researching the free or discounted days for museums and children's centers. Some major museums (or groups of museums) offer free entry days for locals, half-off months, and "kids get in free" days or months. Check out your city's "kids free" options. Some public libraries offer day passes to local museums and other attractions that patrons can check out for free. We like to pair up with friends and share guest passes that are included with some annual museum passes. Many enrichment opportunities, including some amusement parks, have homeschool days with rates for entry that can be as low as 10 percent of the usual cost. Also, research your local neighborhood organizations such as the Boys and Girls Club, the YMCA, and city recreation centers as possibilities for developing a support network and finding additional educational enrichment. When you find a place you want to visit, check its website or contact the venue and ask about homeschool rates, group discounts, and specials.

Boys and Girls Club

Naomi, homeschool parent, single, working full time

Naomi, a homeschooling mother of two children, works at a Boys and Girls Club so that she can manage to homeschool and work at the same time. She knows firsthand the opportunities that a Boys and Girls Club can bring to families with a low budget who need a place for their children to learn from and play with others. The clubs also provide time for parents to get their work done without having to turn to expensive alternatives.

She highlighted this aspect of a San Diego county–based Boys and Girls Club: "For $60 per month, kids can attend as many times as they'd like Monday through Friday from 2:30 to 6:00 p.m. Parents can pick up and drop off anytime, but our twenty-four specialty clubs (sports, 3D printing, digital design, fiber arts, circuit building, Spanish) run from 4:00 to 5:00 p.m., so it's best that they are at least there during that time. The cost is low because we are a nonprofit and we are trying to make the program accessible to everyone."

State-Provided Opportunities

In many states, school districts and charter schools have independent study or homeschool programs (including hybrid options meeting in person for school a few times a week) that allow families to tap into an entire year of free curriculum and monthly meetings with a credentialed teacher. Some programs have resource libraries to borrow teacher's manuals and unused consumable workbooks and science kits. Some states, like Arizona, allow educational tax dollars to follow the student when families choose to homeschool, providing funds for families to use for curriculum, private school tuition/lessons, and activities of their own choosing. Joining homeschool social media groups for your state will help you navigate all the options available to you where you live.

Ways to Avoid Wasting Money

Sometimes we waste money buying curriculum that we do not need, or that does not fit our teaching style or our children's learning-style preferences. Attending a homeschool conference with a full exhibit hall can be a budget-saving decision, even with the registration cost. Exhibit halls are bustling with publishers anxious to show off their curriculum. This is a great opportunity to meet authors or publishers and review potential buys. Check social media groups and ask your homeschool friends for recommendations: gaining insight before you buy will help you make a well-informed purchase.

Challenge Accepted

You can find ways to maintain a small budget while pursuing the homeschool learning of your dreams. Consider it a homeschool lesson in finance: Include your family in this endeavor to tackle the budget. Make a list of priorities and their costs together with your kids. If budget is holding you back, research options while training your brain to view this problem as a gratifying challenge.

Can-Do Assessment to Homeschool on a Budget

- ☐ I can join social media groups focused on free homeschool resources and research the ideas and resources suggested by group members.
- ☐ I can research resources available at local libraries and obtain a card if I do not have one. I have access to transportation to the library.
- ☐ I have access to a computer, tablet, or smartphone to view online videos and download free or inexpensive curriculum or enrichment resources.
- ☐ I have access to transportation to and from enriching experiences, like museums and public parks.
- ☐ I can research my local area to explore free or reduced-cost offers for admission to museums and other attractions.

Part II

Missing Out

"No matter what you do or where you are, you're going to be missing out on something."

—ALAN ARKIN

Many of us have at least a little fear of missing out that drives our decision-making. Some parents are hesitant to homeschool because the traditional school offers opportunities that they fear wouldn't otherwise be available to their child.

While there is definitely some validity to this concern, many of the same types of experiences are available to homeschoolers; they just look a little different or take some creative effort. Here's something to ponder: while *you* may fear your child will miss out, maybe those aren't experiences your child wants anyway.

Chapter 8

Will My Child Miss Out on the School Experience?

MANDI

Do you have FOMO (fear of missing out) about homeschooling? Traditional school experiences *can* be tremendously fun, and we don't want our children to miss out on them. Whether it's celebrations, events, assemblies, sports, the arts, leadership opportunities, clubs, diversity . . . there are a lot of valuable experiences offered in traditional school settings.

I had a blast in school, and maybe you did too. I swam for four years on the varsity swim team, led in student government, dressed up for every theme day, attended dances, and was voted Homecoming Queen. So, I come to these pages with a deep appreciation for the traditional school experience.

As a person with major FOMO, I can confidently tell you: there is no missing out. The homeschooler's experiences are different, but not lacking. This chapter highlights the awesome homeschool experiences awaiting your child.

Celebrations

Let's begin with our favorite classroom fun as kids: the celebrations, classroom parties, and dress-up days. Celebrating the first one hundred days of school in kindergarten is still a momentous occasion in schools. Remember classroom

Thanksgiving meals, holiday pageants, open house, and Mother's Day crafts? Remember the days of decorating brown paper bags with Valentine's stickers, excited for the conversation hearts to fill it up with "you're sweet" and "soulmate"? As the candy hearts say, "trust me," this all can still happen. You make it happen the way you want it and as much or as little as you want.

If you have a co-op, a couple of friends, or a family, you can experience these celebrations.

Celebrations with Our Homeschool Co-op

Since classroom parties were important to me as a child, Jessica and I lead our homeschool co-op in planning celebrations together throughout the year. Our co-op of about forty-five children, ages two to fourteen, has had family Halloween parties, Friendsgiving, a winter holiday movie under the stars, a Valentine's exchange party, a "wear green" treasure hunt, an egg hunt, and more. We've had a wacky hair day paired with Mad Libs fun, an end-of-the-school-year party (which included yearbook signing and a video montage), a couple of poetry teatimes with poem recitations, and book club parties such as a *Black Beauty* rescue-animal farm tour and an *Alice in Wonderland*–inspired Mad Hatter tea party.

The best part? The attendees were children and parents whom we know, love, and invest our time in. The celebrations look different and feel different, but I can assure you that our children are not in want of fun.

Cultural Celebrations

Homeschoolers get to celebrate our own cultural and faith-based holidays with our own family values and traditions. You can celebrate Lunar New Year by going to your city's Chinatown firework fun or feasting with family members all day long—even if it's a weekday! Around Easter time, you can go to the Good Friday church service without needing to pull your kid out of school that day. During Ramadan, your teen can fast during daylight hours with support, surrounded by family (who are also fasting) instead of friends who might not understand at school lunch time.

Celebrating Lunar New Year

JunYee, homeschool parent of six children, California

Homeschool mom JunYee loves to celebrate the Lunar New Year with her six homeschooled children and their extended family. She shared with me that she appreciates the freedom to celebrate late into the night. "We had all our family in from around the world for Chinese New Year one year. My local extended family members didn't let their kids come to the big celebration, because the children had school the next morning. But for us, no biggie. We drove to Los Angeles (a 2.5-hour drive), had a delicious traditional Chinese banquet dinner, and got to see family—without needing to stress about homework or getting back home to make it to school the next morning."

Learning Celebrations

In my home, we celebrate whatever we want! This includes celebrating learning milestones such as these for each child:

- the first one hundred words learned on our spelling list
- when the entire alphabet is written in cursive for the first time
- when a math workbook is finished
- the first individually read chapter book
- the start of a unit study (or the end of one)
- the completion of a newly authored book (my daughter loves to write books)

We celebrate with enthusiastic cheers and excited high-fives, a presentation to the family, a favorite dinner or dessert, or a special family movie night. We celebrate the first day of school with special gifts, new school clothes, signs, and a simple party. We do the same on the last day of school. I cherish these celebrations because I am the one who was part of the struggles, the joys, the failures, and the successes.

Schoolwide Events and Assemblies

Whether it's inspiring assemblies, pep rallies, carnivals, book fairs, or ice cream socials, schoolwide events can provide opportunities for growth and fun. A number of these experiences can be re-created within a homeschool group.

Larger group activities are harder to replicate, so my family solved that problem by signing up for our homeschool charter school's half-day enrichment program. Supported by the parent leadership club, the program offered fun events like an Usborne book fair, pizza parties, assemblies, and an end-of-year carnival (with inflatables) with special guests. Now we have experiences like these with our co-op.

Prom-dress shopping was both fun and stressful, but always a wonderful bonding event with my parents when I was in high school. In traditional school, not everyone gets invited to prom, but with homeschooling, invites are not required! Your child can "dress shop" too—for a family dance or the homeschool prom. Our homeschool group hosts an annual Spring Fling family dance, with parents in the roles of disc jockey, emcee, photographer, dessert table hostess, decorator, and crafter, sometimes charging a small fee per family to pay for costs. Even if there are just a few families, sweet memories dance their way into all of our hearts as we limbo!

When it comes to prom with a small group, you can be uber-creative. Ever heard of a prom that includes appetizers on a train, a fancy dinner, a ferry ride to a nearby island, and a live play? We have! When Jessica was in high school, her homeschool group's parents planned a "formal" for about thirty teenagers. What a great inspiration!

Sports

Matching gear, school pride, bus rides, awards banquets, sportsmanship lessons, teamwork, fitness, pageantry, and mascots . . . should I keep going? I cannot say enough about the benefits that school sports offer in terms of building up your child as an individual and as a member of a community. As a former UCLA swimmer, I get it! I lived it!

Some experiences related to school sports are not replicable when you homeschool, but the most important aspects are. Club sports, YMCA recreational sports, dance schools, local leagues and franchises, and neighborhood gym sports are available for learning and competing in sports. Did you know that there are homeschool companies and organizations that provide these opportunities for all ages as well? These sports groups include gear, team pride, sportsmanship lessons, fitness, and character development. No, there likely won't be pep rallies, Friday night lights, or homecoming royalty, but that's part of what you weigh in your homeschool cost-benefit analysis.

Many student athletes compete on teams outside of their school experience. I did, and most of my friends in various sports did, too. Many sports are not offered in traditional schools, so students attending those schools would participate in out-of-school leagues, which are open to kids no matter their education settings. You can check out your local recreation centers, club teams, and sports program vendors.

Sports at the Public School

Sometimes the traditional school is the only way to experience a specific sport. Some public schools authorize homeschoolers to participate in their sports offerings, and all you need to do to start the process is contact the coach. The availability of this option depends on state and district rules. Whether or not your district allows this type of participation is something to consider in your decision-making process.

Some states have adopted equal access athletic bills, or "Tim Tebow" laws, granting homeschool athletes access to sports programs at public schools. There are arguments for and against these bills, but if you want to homeschool your children *and* have them compete on a public school's sports team, you may be able to do that. If sports opportunities are your hesitation, remember that there are many different kinds of ways to participate.

Flexibility for an Ice Skater

Alicia, homeschool parent, Arizona

Alicia, in her fourth year homeschooling her sixth grade daughter, shares how she prioritizes sports: "My daughter is super into figure skating. She competes in Ladies Singles, Ice Dancing, and Ballroom Dance. She is passionate about her sport and trains around thirty-five to forty hours per week.

"This is our fourth year homeschooling. Homeschooling gave us the flexibility needed for her to train full time, spend time with family and friends, and still have time for school.

"I think the best part has been her ability to learn on her own time. She doesn't like to sit still very long, so she works thirty minutes, and then gets some exercise in, then works another thirty minutes, and then gets more exercise in. Homeschooling also gave her the opportunity to explore other interests, make many friends, it allowed us to travel more, turn learning into game time, and now we get to have deep conversations about life."

Performing Arts and Fine Arts

Many of us learned to play the recorder in elementary school; it was a rite of passage. Music and art were once a major component of schooling, complete with weekly lessons from a music teacher, art projects and electives, class or school choir, square dance or cotillion, band, marching band in high school, theater group, and other performance opportunities. Though less prevalent than they used to be, these opportunities still exist in many schools (for free or at low cost).

As a homeschooled middle schooler, Jessica made special arrangements with the public middle school to participate in its band program. She played flute in the concert band and saxophone in the jazz band. She was on campus only for those classes and attended competitions and celebrations with her bandmates. Often, children pursue their art, music, and performing passions outside of school in late afternoons or evenings. However, homeschooled children have the option of taking lessons and practicing during the day.

One year, our children participated in a half-day, weekly homeschool arts program. The program's students, ages six to twelve, worked on scripts, set design, art, performance techniques, choreography, and more. At the end of each semester, we attended their performances. The fall semester produced *The Nutcracker* as a musical, and the spring semester performed Shakespeare's *A Midsummer Night's Dream*, with homemade costumes and an Old Globe Theatre art project. Your children can have these types of unique experiences customized to their interests; you just have to look for opportunities in your own area.

Are lessons beyond your budget? The internet has numerous wonderful lessons available for free. You can curate videos ahead of time and create your own playlists. The Kennedy Center and Mo Willems, author of the Elephant and Piggie book series, offer a free fifteen-episode series online about how to draw all sorts of animals. The series includes other creative art ideas too. It can be even more fun to tap into your homeschool community to see if any adults (or older siblings) have art or music skills that they can share.

Student Body Leadership

Future leaders unite! Traditional school offers a great opportunity for children and teens to test out and practice leadership skills as part of their classes, student government, or clubs. Leadership opportunities during school years help children evaluate whether a potential career in leadership could be a good fit.

Although it's on a much smaller scale, homeschooled children can lead among friends from the neighborhood, in enrichment courses, or as part of co-ops or faith-based communities. On a sports team? If your child is chosen as team captain or social/culture captain, that's a clue to find other ways for them to lead when the season ends. The YMCA offers a program called Youth and Government for teens to experience a youth version of a race to governorship. Also, you can search online for vendors offering mock trial experiences, speech and debate lessons and competitions, leadership camps, and public speaking institutes. Many of these vendors offer camps and courses during the summer months.

Leadership Love

While homeschooled in high school, Jessica was part of a leadership group. She recounts: "My community of homeschoolers hosted a leadership group called the 'Independent Study Student Union,' or 'I.S.S.U.' as we loved to call it. I ran for and was elected secretary during my second year, while the boy I'd later marry was the sergeant-at-arms keeping order during meetings. We organized service projects, put on community banquets with silent auctions to benefit a local charity, worked the annual Fourth of July fair, and planned other fun experiences."

Clubs and Groups

Clubs are a great way to unite children and teens who share a common interest. Clubs can be formed through community groups or joined at local businesses, like the Pokémon club at game stores. Libraries also offer a wonderful array of opportunities such as chess clubs, book clubs, writing groups, second-language story hours, weekly art classes, and even family bingo clubs. Check out the libraries, YMCA, local recreation centers, city parks, and Boys and Girls Clubs in your area for a calendar of meet-ups.

As our personal community of homeschoolers has grown, clubs have organically started popping up. A seven-year-old homeschool friend of ours loves crafts, so she created a monthly kids craft club and designed the crafts and led the instruction. Our co-op hosts three book clubs, one for teens, one for tweens, and one for younger readers. It also hosts a *Pokémon GO* club, an etiquette club, a yearbook committee, and a drama club. My children participate in a homeschool robotics club too. These clubs have been an amazing gift to our children's educational experience.

Diversity

In the homeschool world, we share a bond with diverse families spanning various cultures, ethnicities, and creeds. We connect based on our passion to raise our children differently than the norm, and we share a conviction about the value of being autonomous and independent of requirements to educate our children in a specific way.

That being said, the spectrum of diversity depends on one's geographical region, and not everyone has the opportunity to be enveloped by a rich variety of cultures, religions, political opinions, and nationalities, no matter our school choice. Homeschoolers can meet people different from themselves by enjoying cultural and faith-based festivals, participating in sports or dance lessons, reaching out to people at outsourced activities, and connecting with others at homeschool conferences. (See chapter 10 for more about diversity.)

We Make It Happen

In a homeschool lifestyle, for most of these wonderful experiences, we need to be the point person. We, ourselves, make it happen. We plan opportunities and customize them to match our children's interests and passions and to allow them to be with the people they love most. Our role in these activities is much larger than it would ever need to be in a classroom-based school. For some, this can be intimidating. For others, it's an adventure. Which is it for you?

If you are not the type of person to seek out opportunities or create them yourself, attach yourself to someone who is. When there is an event, show up. If you are asked to be part of a homeschool group, enthusiastically say, "Yes!" You might not find the perfect fit right away, but if you want these enriching experiences for your children, you need to open yourself up to join in when invited.

Or, we can decide to skip it, take a break, and focus for a time on the joys of being together as a family in a peaceful, no-frills, home-based lifestyle. It's our own choice. The best part? We get to be there for all of it.

Can-Do Assessment to Create Experiences

❏ I can make a list of the activities and celebrations traditional schools typically offer and choose the five that are most important to me or my child to implement this next school year.

❏ I feel comfortable researching or asking friends for recommendations for companies to explore my child's interests. I can search for online videos or classes.

❏ If my child shows interest in leadership, I am willing to help them pursue their interest by designing and leading one club, lesson, activity, or adventure for our family or homeschool friends.

❏ I can take my children to cultural festivals, invite people for playdates, and reach out to others to expose my children to people different from themselves.

❏ I can look for a nearby homeschool group that is open for new members. If not, I can make a list of families I know that might be interested in connecting as a community on a regular basis and plan the first activity for and with them. (They don't have to be homeschoolers.)

Chapter 9

Will My Child Miss Out on Community?

MANDI

Picture this: cheerleaders, marching band, and families eating snack-bar nachos under the Friday night lights. . . this shared experience connecting with people we know and love depicts the immeasurable value we feel for our community. As traditional schoolers, many of us grew up together practicing our lines during late-night theater rehearsals or debating marijuana legalization at debate club tournaments. The key word here is *together*. Community can be a huge gift to families in traditional school life; we have many memories of such times that we still get nostalgic about. That feeling of community, that sense of belonging, can be powerful and enriching. Many of us don't want our children to miss out on that.

Good news! If you decide to homeschool, you don't have to miss out on the vital gifts that being part of a community brings. Jessica was homeschooled through middle school and high school, yet she has a community with whom she shared her teen years and made her own set of amazing memories. Homeschool communities are simply formed in a different way than traditional school communities, based on different experiences and commonalities. We might not bond during large-scale sports rallies or all-night study sessions—but with time, initiative, and intention to reach out to others, we can ensure that our children experience the joy that comes from being part of a community.

92

What Is Community?

Community has long been understood as a group of people who are unified around something they have in common. We agree with the general definition, but we think there's more. There is the intangible factor that community brings to our lives, going beyond commonality: a sense of belonging. It is the sense of security that comes from knowing that we have a group of people who care about us, and we care about them, and we bring each other joy. We all want that for our children.

New York City Teacher of the Year and author John Taylor Gatto observes, "Communities are collections of families and friends who find major meaning in extending the family association to a band of honorary brothers and sisters. They are complex relationships of commonality and obligation that generalize to others beyond the perimeter of the homestead" (Gatto 2017, 63). When we form a community, we are basically extending the family unit. What a glorious concept!

What We Love about Community

We enjoy these benefits of being part of an intentional community:

- connection as families through a shared identity and purpose
- common values and behaviors
- engagement with diverse backgrounds, races, and belief systems
- commitment to each other with a long-term vision
- nurturing friendship growth with memorable experiences together
- support, advice, and resources for pursuing shared interests and passions

The Gift of a Homeschooling Community

As homeschoolers, we are gifted with the opportunity to play a bigger role in building community. Through meeting as families and tailoring our time together to our interests and needs, we can devote time to finding kinship and connection for our entire family.

- Family connection—All members of the community can connect on a deep level, not only the children, but the entire family.

- Tailored connection—We and our children can choose a unique community tailored to some of our interests and needs.

- Schedule optimization—We get to play an active role in ensuring the schedule is the best use of our time, set by us and our small homeschool group.

- Parent-child connection—Best of all, we are part of this community with our children in a significant way, caring for their friends, too, as a participator, coach, or mentor. It's up to us.

Living the Homeschool Dream

Marie, homeschool parent and business owner in the manufacturing field, California

Marie compared her traditional school education with her husband's homeschooling journey. She wrote, "I met my husband when we were sixteen. I went to the public high school and he was homeschooled. I was an honors kid with a great GPA, but when talking about things we had both learned in school, I was shocked at how little I knew about things I thought I had a good grasp on. History, literature, calculus—I knew the broad strokes, but he understood the details. I came to understand that while I was good at memorizing facts to pass a test, he had mastered the same subjects in a way that was never expected in my classes. I was jealous that his education was more robust than mine, while also giving him ample free time to pursue his hobbies and spend time with friends. One of the major highlights of his homeschooling life was his homeschool community, particularly his history co-op. They studied time periods wearing period dress and bonded over interesting facts, with every mom sharing the load and forming friendships as well.

> "When we had our own kids, it went without saying that we would homeschool them. I dreamed of giving them an education and community like the one my husband was fortunate to have, which I was so jealous of as a teenager. Now with one teenager of our own and another [child] on the cusp of adolescence, we have never once regretted our decision. Homeschooling our children is quite literally a dream come true."

Homeschoolers Are Not Alone

Homeschooling is not as rare as it once was. A spring 2019 study showed that there were 2.5 million homeschooled students in the United States, or 3 to 4 percent of school-age children (NHERI 2023), which is more than double the number of homeschooled students from twenty years earlier (Bielick, Chandler, and Broughman 2001). A study by the National Center for Educational Statistics from 2012 and 2016 shows that no matter where we live, be it city, suburb, town, or rural area, homeschoolers are all around to share our adventures (US Department of Education 2019). Since 2020, the numbers have continued to grow.

What about finding people who homeschool who are like you? The research indicates that you will. The demographics of homeschoolers closely match the demographics of students in traditional public schools across income levels, race and ethnicity, parent education levels, and other categories (Coalition for Responsible Home Education 2017).

An Abundance of Communities

Many types of homeschool communities may already exist near you, whether they are casual co-ops, formal co-ops, micro-schools, themed groups, collectives, or enrichment programs. The homeschooling world is bigger than many people think—and there are all different kinds of communities. The formation and intention of these communities varies widely. Homeschooling communities might have grown from groups of casual friends or adventure seekers, people looking for group learning environments, or other interest-led connections. Requirements and levels of commitment vary as well. You can learn more by investigating your options.

As mentioned previously, there are communities, organizations, businesses, and charter schools (in some states) that exist solely for homeschooler connection and learning. Some companies and organizations guide homeschoolers in classroom environments focusing on particular skills or academics, like robotics, STEM skills, science labs, or second language development. Some classes meet once a week for specific academics, and others meet more frequently. Homeschool charter schools in some states offer a series of drop-off days for classes focused on a specific topic or elective. With these opportunities, you can dive into a community and build long-term relationships too.

Will My Child Fit In?

We all long for our children to grow up in a community that provides them with a sense of belonging; it is a valid concern to wonder if your children will fit in among homeschoolers. Give it time. Finding the community that is right for your child is a significant endeavor.

Homeschool communities serve varying purposes and appeal to different types of people. You shouldn't get discouraged when you encounter a homeschooling group or two that wouldn't be right for your children. You may have to try a few different communities to find a good fit. In the meantime, it's a relief to know that you get to choose the community best suited for your own family.

If You Build It, Homeschoolers Will Come

If existing communities are not a fit for you or your child, you can build a community yourself. Homeschool families can be found online or at sports programs, at local library activities, at church functions, on the apartment elevator, or on a walk to the corner park. Community starts with meeting people and making friends who share your values and want to create similar experiences.

Teen Huddle

As our children became tweens and teens, they expressed a desire to have a specialized community with kids ages eleven to fourteen. They wanted a time together where they could connect with other kids their age without the distractions of their younger siblings. Our co-op parents listened and agreed, so we built the "Teen Huddle" club, a community of homeschool tweens and teens and their parents who plan monthly connecting and memorable hangouts. Sometimes they are casual times with games, pool play, or an ice cream buffet, and other times they are very organized, such as a teen-friendly pizzeria-themed murder mystery party. (We bought one online, and all the parents chipped in to defray the cost.) Our older children love this community.

My eleven-year-old shared this: "Teen Huddle is one of my favorite things I do. I love being able to hang out with my friends. My favorite activity by far has been the Murder Mystery Party. It was so fun seeing how everybody took on their characters and acted them out. It was also hilarious seeing what some people's scripts were, like one of the kids had to confess his love to another and sing a song about it. That night will be something my friends and I joke about for years. Another one of my favorites was the pool party. We had so much fun making up games on the diving board, tossing floaties onto each other like the game Horseshoe, and jumping on the trampoline. I look forward to every Teen Huddle."

Our Homeschool Group Experience

Our homeschool group has evolved and grown together organically. Jessica and I met through our daughters' dance class and began the group. We invited the homeschooling families from that class and have since added other homeschooling friends. These friends invited their friends to our group over time. Over five years, we grew from six families to eighteen.

We Bond Over Unique Learning Experiences

Our members have experienced a science fair, a mock election, strawberry picking, a pumpkin patch visit, a camping weekend, museum tours, a steel drum lesson, pasta-making, art lessons, obstacle courses, yearbook parties, and more. Activities like field trips and living history experiences are more fun with a group of friends. Or, if we can get a homeschool group discount, we know to call up our co-op—the more people we bring, the cheaper and merrier the activity is!

We Have a Diverse Homeschool Community

Our co-op became diverse over time, and our members span the gamut of political beliefs, religions, cultures, and more. This happened organically by building caring and accepting relationships with the people around us. We found connection and commonalities with people when we invested our time and we have grown to appreciate the sparks that make us different. The conviction and passion to homeschool is the driving force that connects homeschoolers in this lifestyle. (For more about diversity, see chapter 10.)

We Serve Others

We want our kids to practice thinking beyond their own interests and considering the needs of others and how they can help. Generosity can be shown in at least seven ways. It can be more than giving money or belongings; it also includes giving one's time, attention, influence, words, and thoughts, which are ways kids can really get involved (Generous Family 2023). We want that kindness to spill over into all facets of life, but we all need to practice.

So, as a group, we try to serve our community annually in one of these seven ways. Examples include making homemade Thanksgiving cards for the residents of an assisted care facility, singing holiday carols and making ornaments for the residents of a memory care facility, making blankets for animals at a local Humane Society shelter, and raising funds to purchase farming animals for families in developing countries through Heifer International.

The life and relationship skills that we develop through our co-op are the best learning experiences we offer our children in our entire homeschooling journey. You can build a co-op too, starting with one other family, and adding more families over time like we did.

Community Needs You

Building or participating in a community does take effort. Is that something you are prepared to put intention toward? If so, you can do this.

Homeschooling is a parenting decision. As the parent, your job when at extracurricular events is to reach out to others so that the events become more than just enrichment; they become connecting moments that build community. There are many resources for building a group or joining one that you can investigate online or by posting in social media homeschooling groups. The key ingredients are investing yourself and committing to togetherness.

Community Takes Time, Energy, and Heart, but It Is Worth It

Finding community is one of the most important pieces of advice we give to new homeschoolers. Community looks different for every family based on their own social needs and desire for support. Maybe you prefer to be the leader and organizer of a community, or maybe you prefer to be part of one. Whether you join an existing community or start your own—it is worth it!

Can-Do Assessment to Be Part of a Community

❏ I am able to research the types of communities (co-ops, interest-based, activity-based, etc.) available and then determine what kind of community we need.

❏ I am willing to reach out to others to inquire about opportunities to join a community that interests me or my children.

❏ I have access to research online or on social media to find opportunities for homeschool meet-ups.

❏ I have space in my weekly or monthly schedule to invest time in a community.

❏ I am willing to meet new people and join in on new experiences.

Chapter 10

Will My Child Miss Out on Diversity?

MANDI

Some people think homeschooled children miss out on knowing people different from themselves. Many groups of people who gather together can be homogenous, formed around culture, race, religion, politics, socioeconomic status, age, gender, and so on; this includes the traditional school setting. Whatever our schooling choice, we can all work hard to expose our children to people different from themselves, in order to help them lead more enriched, empathetic, and kind lives. We can help our children broaden their perspectives and develop open-mindedness by ensuring they learn about the experiences of others.

Dispelling Some Common Myths

Do you wonder if your family will fit into the homeschool community? There are stereotypes of what a homeschooling family looks like, but homeschooling has actually become more diverse over the years. Let's explore this more fully.

Race and Ethnicity

In the United States, homeschooling was disproportionately White up until 2017. As of 2022, however, the proportions are more similar across racial/ethnic groups (Duvall 2022):

- 9.9 percent of White families homeschool

- 10.3 percent of Black families homeschool

- 8.9 percent of Hispanic, Latino, or Spanish-origin families homeschool

- 8.01 percent of Asian families homeschool

- 13.7 percent of families of other races homeschool

Socioeconomic Status

Homeschool families have historically been as diverse in their income as public school families (McQuiggan and Megra 2017; Coalition for Responsible Home Education 2017).

Jessica and I see this diversity within our co-op. A few of us rely on a single income, have to be very careful with spending, and are living month to month. Some of the homeschool parents in our group have additional part-time jobs to bring in a bit of extra income. Other families have higher incomes or two full-time salaries that afford them more financial freedom. As a group, we are considerate of all our co-op families when we plan events with fees in order to include everyone.

Religion and Politics

We have learned from our experience, the communities we've met, and testimonials we've heard throughout the country that homeschoolers are diverse in religious beliefs and political affiliations as well. For example, our co-op of eighteen families includes people who are (or were raised as) agnostics, atheists, Buddhists, Christians, Muslims, Democrats, Republicans, Libertarians, and Independents. Our children are exposed to families with differences in beliefs, opinions, and thoughts. No matter the make-up of our communities, we all have the freedom to explore and learn about various systems of belief.

We All Need Diversity

For me, this is my favorite aspect of homeschooling. If you are worried that a homeschooling life will limit diversity exposure, we want to share some ideas that have worked for us. You can even try a few of them before making the choice to homeschool, to see if these types of activities would work for your family.

Learn Together

Learning together as a family and with others, using thoughtfully developed resources, connects our children to learning about diversity in memorable ways.

Conduct a Mock Election

In the fall of 2020, our co-op conducted a mock election with fictional characters to learn about and discuss politics and the election process. It was incredibly fun to teach dozens of kids the voting process, and we saw the diversity of thought and opinion within our own group. Our kids had to learn to wait their turn, share their opinions with kindness and respect, and stand firm on their convictions. We were able to apply the learning in our homes to discuss the election happening in real life.

Read Together

If you've been reading this book cover to cover, you already know that reading together can make a huge impact on a family, including developing new perspectives and an understanding about those different from oneself. Reading a range of diverse books together and discussing the differing perspectives can enrich our lives no matter our school choice. In the picture book *Malala's Magic Pencil* by Malala Yousafzai, the author shares the importance of civil rights for all people as she perseveres through fear and suffering. As a family, we enjoy learning together by reading the Who Was? series. As we read an installment aloud, we discuss the historical figures, the challenges that they faced, and their impact on the world. A classic book that I loved reading to my kids was *Have You Filled a Bucket Today? A Guide to Daily Happiness for Kids*, by Carol McCloud. This book uses the metaphor of a bucket, showing that when we fill one another's buckets with encouragement and kindness, our buckets are filled too. I love this book's call to fill others' buckets no matter who they are. With our co-op we read this book, and then we practiced filling each other's buckets using encouragement coins.

Watch Documentaries

Various cultures, family structures, and personal struggles come to life in documentaries. My family has watched *Mad Hot Ballroom*, *Spellbound*, *Imba Means Sing*, and *Living on One Dollar*. I've seen my children's faces fill with fascination and heard their thoughts about their learning bubble up for days afterward. We recommend previewing documentaries in advance to ensure a topic is appropriate for your child's development level and to prepare questions to discuss as a family afterward.

Study Deeply

Homeschooling infused with earnest study of the religions, mythology, and folktales of other cultures can greatly enrich people's lives. We explore how we still see evidence of these historic beliefs around us. My kids love lifting the flaps on our Usborne *See Inside World Religions* book, and *The Usborne Encyclopedia of World Religions* is a good book for older students to enjoy. Chronicle Books has a beautifully illustrated series of books offering tales from around the world like *Tales of East Africa* and *Celtic Tales: Fairy Tales and Stories of Enchantment*.

Cook and Craft Together

Sometimes, my family enjoys special nights when we make recipes that represent popular foods from different countries. The online cooking club Raddish Kids offers recipe boxes for various countries. We've signed up for other subscription box kits that help us appreciate various countries and cultures through recipes and crafts (which we use to decorate for family dinner). Some examples are Universal Yums and Atlas Crate by KiwiCo.

Learn a Language as a Family

My family started with American Sign Language when our children were little to help our nonverbal kids communicate. Then, in early elementary, we tried Mandarin; but after one year, we decided it was too hard for us, so we switched to Latin. After two years of Latin, we started learning Spanish through Duolingo to prepare for a trip to Ensenada, Mexico. My middle school daughter was so committed to learning Spanish that she completed a 190-day streak with her Duolingo lessons! We loved this family challenge.

Experience Together

We enjoy making memories by attending cultural festivals. These festivals often include food, dancing, traditional clothing, music, and a great time. We also keep track of holidays celebrated by other cultures and spend time on those days learning about their meanings and the related traditions.

My husband, who earned advanced degrees in history, thoroughly enjoyed a two-week historical tour of Israel one fall. He arrived home with a wealth of knowledge, souvenirs, and relics to share with us. His experience was incredibly helpful as we studied ancient Israel and the Israelites that winter. For enrichment, we used the Ancient Israelites kit from *History Unboxed*, which included a shofar. To help our children understand the beauty of Hanukkah, we celebrated our own version that December in a respectful and honoring way. It was an illuminating evening in more ways than one with candles, traditional Jewish food, and instruments.

Meet and Develop Relationships with People

Diversity can be all around us whether we are part of a dance school, chess club, art class, or sports league. We can seize these opportunities by inviting families to a BBQ at a local park to get to know them better. We can join or design a co-op that includes families with different perspectives, racial identities, philosophies, religions, ages, neighborhoods, interests, and economic levels. We can attend community events with the goal of meeting new people from various cultures and backgrounds, and form new connections.

We need to be open and willing to share ourselves. Others can learn from us as well. Every person has a gift of experience, perspective, and culture to offer, so let's be open to sharing ours. Full diversity immersion can truly happen when we and our children form long-lasting relationships with people whose cultural backgrounds and life experiences are different from ours. We will find common ground that we can connect on—sometimes it's simply a passion for parenting.

Freedom to Worship

Samira, homeschool parent and full-time lawyer, California

Samira immigrated to the United States from Afghanistan in the late 1980s and attended public school. As a Muslim in middle school, she found it difficult to follow her convictions during Ramadan. She shared this with me: "When I was younger I would go to school fasting because I wanted to fast for Ramadan along with my parents. My parents didn't force me, but I remember not having any energy to learn in class or do physical sports. And no one understood because at the time Islam and Afghanistan were so foreign to people. It seemed like people I encountered locally weren't aware of Middle Easterners in general and had no clue about them, their culture, or their religion until 9/11. Now, as a homeschool parent, I am thankful that my children will have the freedom to celebrate with whom and how they want."

Jessica and I love the diversity in our homeschool community. Samira and her family are some of our closest friends. We love her example, because as homeschoolers we can choose to learn from Samira and her kids during the school day. Our children learn to appreciate differing perspectives, approaches, and lifestyles through our homeschool group. Our community is made up of families on all sides of the political and economic spectrum, with various faiths, philosophies, and home cultures. They have rich family histories in China, Japan, Vietnam, Latin America, the Middle East, and Europe, and we have bilingual families who speak Spanish and Farsi. Our children are learning to navigate social situations with about forty-five children of diverse ages (babies to teenagers), interests, and temperaments.

Travel Together

We can experience the diversity of the world in our own cities. In many metropolitan areas, we don't need to go far to find a new cultural experience. We can try local mom-and-pop restaurants and sample foods that are new to us. We can take walking tours of cities or local communities and visit historical sites to learn about how they were founded and developed. When visiting a farmer's market or farm stand, we can talk with the farmers and learn from them.

Take a day trip to various art museums or cultural heritage museums, and ask the docents about the artists and displays. Choose historical figures and study their backgrounds, talents, and impact; then visit sites that were a part of their journey. Take a bike, train, or plane to places that teach about an area's indigenous people. A few years ago our homeschool co-op traveled the world together without ever boarding a plane—by learning about a different country every month with hands-on activities, food, and experiences.

Cultural Memories We've Made

A few years ago, we visited the first Spanish mission in what is now California, where we learned about the Kumeyaay people and Junipero Serra's missionary work during the 1700s. Through primary sources, mission tours, and educational books and booklets, we explored various points of view about Serra's controversial legacy. This content informed my children's opinions when they wrote essays about Spain's engagement with the indigenous people in the region.

When my family traveled to Alaska, we toured Totem Bight State Historical Park in Ketchikan while learning about the Tlingit Nation. Then we shared a canoe to a small island, learning about their transportation on site. At a Tlingit heritage museum, we witnessed a beautiful Tlingit song and traditional dance and watched a film about Tlingit history and culture.

Another time, we went to San Francisco and toured Chinatown with a good friend who immigrated from China when she was five. She helped us practice Mandarin greetings and questions (although most people in that area spoke Cantonese). The shopkeepers were amused and smiled upon hearing our attempts at the dialect, and one man gave us some tips for greetings in Cantonese. My six-year-old daughter bought traditional Chinese clothing with her own money and wore them with pride the rest of the day.

When we homeschool, our exposure to diverse people is not limited to our local neighborhoods, because we get to make time to venture into other neighborhoods and form friendships beyond district lines. Start off by trying one of our ideas and see where it takes you. A homeschooling lifestyle could be the very thing that brings more diversity to your family's life.

Can-Do Assessment to Add Diversity

☐ I can pick one type of activity that will build my child's cultural awareness and open-mindedness, and regularly incorporate it into our life.

☐ I am open to new relationships and experiences and can reach out to others and help my children do the same.

☐ I am willing to share our family's perspective with others in mutual appreciation for our similarities and differences.

☐ I can find my own fun in learning something new and different.

Chapter 11

Will My Child Miss Out on the Academic Classroom?

JESSICA

Many parents have shared their concern that homeschooled students will miss out on academic opportunities typically available in public and private traditional schools, in terms of either the subject matter or the classroom experience. This is a valid concern; however, it's clear that kids can learn outside of classrooms, whether in their homes or on the go. We can tell you with confidence that homeschoolers can experience strong academic achievement, high test scores, and enriching academic opportunities.

The Proof Is in the Test Scores

Several studies compared test scores of homeschooled and public-schooled students, and the results are good news for homeschooling. Research over the past two decades shows that homeschoolers score higher on standardized academic achievement tests than their public-schooled counterparts (National Home Education Research Institute 2023; Treleaven 2022). While the point is not who scores higher, this evidence should assure you that homeschooled students can and do perform well on achievement tests. (For additional information on high school academics and college preparedness, see chapter 16.) Achievement is only one part of this conversation, though. There are other issues to consider.

Academic Curriculum

As discussed in chapter 1, access to curriculum is abundant for homeschoolers. We can choose to homeschool with a curriculum used by traditional schools. Or we can choose a curriculum designed for homeschoolers. Some homeschool curriculum is robust and meets state standards. (See chapter 15 if you worry about your child falling behind.) Curriculum is available in book form and online, making it easy to fit our needs. There are also curriculum materials, unit studies, and enrichment resources designed for different learning styles, interests, and preferences. Homeschooling allows us to tailor curriculum to our children's needs and interests and delve more deeply into specific subjects or explore alternative educational approaches.

High School Psychology Course

Valorie, homeschool parent of five children (now graduated)

Valorie explained that she allowed her kids to come up with their own course of study in order to support their interests. Here is one example she gave us. "One year my daughter wanted to learn more about brain computer interfaces (BCI). She read an article about how BCI can be used to help with mental illness. So . . . the big question was: Can I design a BCI that will help with symptoms of anxiety and ADHD?

"We bought a model online and then she designed some experiments. They failed. . . So, what she ended up doing was a semester-long deep dive into research on things that do help symptoms of anxiety. She created a brochure, wrote numerous journal articles, interviewed clinicians, and then designed another experiment on the effects of exercise on anxiety. Bingo! By the end of that semester, she had written four really solid research papers, learned a whole lot about mental health, and gained some valuable people skills. I tracked the hours and assignments, and on her transcript that credit shows up as Lab-based Psychology."

Access to Resources

Traditional schools often have well-established infrastructures, specialized teachers for various subjects, and resources such as science labs, music programs, or athletic facilities. They also have computer labs, school libraries, college admissions counseling, and more. Homeschooling requires us to be proactive in finding resources and opportunities outside the home, such as community classes, co-ops, or online courses, as well as reading books or attending online workshops or homeschool conferences. If access to resources is a challenge, below are some possible solutions.

Libraries

This isn't the first time we've talked about how great local libraries can be. Depending on the library, you may have access to computers (some allow users to check out computers for a full year), 3-D printers, classes, rare books, tutoring, and other research-related resources. And don't underestimate the expertise of librarians; they are a treasure trove of recommendations.

In-Person Enrichment

Researching the enrichment options locally can spark or develop your children's interests. During my high school years, a local science teacher taught biology, chemistry, and physics out of my friend's garage to homeschooled students. We paid for his services (which were affordable) and experienced enhanced learning from being in a science classroom and lab setting.

Weekend programs are options for those with busy weekday schedules. Mandi's daughter attended a veterinary class on a Sunday at a local animal shelter. She practiced sutures on a banana, bandaged simulated wounds, and even learned about CPR for dogs. Many areas have enrichment facilities for homeschoolers offering courses and electives such as art, music, and language programs; STEM labs; game design, engineering, and robotics classes; cooking courses; filmmaking; world history lessons through Minecraft; sports; sewing; and tutoring.

Online Enrichment

Similar to in-person enrichment, online programs like Khan Academy and Outschool offer classes by specialized teachers that may meet the need for tutoring, electives, labs, test prep courses, and life skills. Through Outschool, Mandi's daughter enjoyed a weekly literature-based writing class for fans of the Warriors book series and enjoyed numerous rabbit care courses to prepare for her new pet. A co-op friend took weekly Harry Potter–themed classes for a few quarters on Outschool, learning about molecules, chemical versus physical reactions, thermodynamics, the periodic table, foreshadowing, tone, and ethics.

Public School Independent Study Programs

Many public school districts offer an independent study program (ISP) to students. While some parents might say this is not technically "homeschooling," it is a great high school option that allows students access to Advanced Placement® (AP), honors, and International Baccalaureate® (IB) classes, as well as the school's resources, with the benefits of working independently at home. Often, ISP students are able to participate in on-campus events as well, so students get some of the benefits of both schooling scenarios.

Charter Schools and Other Options

California seems to lead the states in diverse public charter school offerings. In San Diego County alone, there are about 130 public charter schools, around 40 of which offer only non-classroom-based learning. The remaining 90 have physical campuses, but many offer independent study programs (California Department of Education, n.d.). Some offer hybrid programs that include on-campus elective classes on certain days of the week.

Colorado boasts public charter schools such as Colorado Early Colleges and the Options Program that allow flexibility to homeschoolers. Missouri has private "university model" schools that allow homeschooled students to pay tuition and take classes on campus a couple days a week and homeschool the other days. We highlight these states because friends and family in them have shared with us their gratitude for these programs.

Each state's opportunities differ, so research at the Home School Legal Defense Association (HSLDA) website and your state's department of education website, as well as at your local school district. You never know what opportunities are available nearby.

Community College/Dual Enrollment

Community college courses can be an option for homeschooled students. Community colleges set their own parameters for accepting minors as "special admits," but most allow it.

The summer I was thirteen years old, I enrolled at my local community college to take a dance class. I was a bit surprised that I had to read a book on jazz theory and take a written midterm and final, but the class was so much fun that I continued to take dance classes at the college through high school. At age fourteen and in eighth grade, I was permitted to take math and English courses on campus.

Once I was in high school, I took advantage of the dual enrollment program that most community colleges offer to high schoolers. This allowed me to take courses and simultaneously earn high school and college credit. I took biology lab, concert band, and many other courses that complemented my at-home work.

Academic Classroom and Group Learning Experiences

One concern I had during my daughter's early homeschooling days was the classroom-style or group learning she would miss out on by being homeschooled. Specifically, experiences such as book discussions with peers, voting on which class pet to get, spelling bees, and show-and-tell days.

During our first homeschool year, my fears were soothed once my daughter started taking a dance class. I realized that group learning could happen within the dance class. As an extra bonus, that's where and when I met other families who were homeschooling or planning to homeschool, and I realized that I could create academic experiences with these families outside of the dance class.

An academic classroom experience was possible; it just looked different and required more of me.

Co-Ops

Co-ops offer excellent opportunities for group learning. Mandi and I specifically designed our co-op to include the fun of having a group with which to learn and grow. With poetry readings, biography presentations, science fair projects, polls and graphing experiences, field trips, and so much more, we ensure our children do not miss out on the academic benefits of a classroom. While our "classroom" may be the park or home where we meet, our co-op kids regularly experience the best of what a classroom offers.

Enrichment Classes

As described in chapter 1, enrichment classes—anything that enhances the quality or value of education—whether in person or online, can offer group learning experiences as well. These classes are excellent places for children to meet and interact with other students while learning a subject or studying a common interest together.

Academic Clubs and Competitions

Some of us want the math Olympiads, academic decathlons, science fairs, spelling bees, robotics clubs, Model UN activities, and debate teams for our children. How do we offer those experiences when homeschooling? They're still available to us—it's our job to find them or create them.

The Scripps National Spelling Bee allows homeschool groups or co-ops to register and compete just as they allow public and private schools to register. A mom in our co-op formed a LEGO® robotics team by registering with FIRST LEGO League. She had no prior knowledge about how it all worked, but she learned along the way, and with her efforts and the team's commitment, the team advanced after their very first local competition! Many academic clubs and teams exist outside of traditional schools; we simply have to do the work of finding them.

Internship Options

Sharon, homeschool parent and administrator and art teacher at a music studio, California

Sharon, homeschool mother of two teens, shared about her children's experiences with internships. She wrote, "Internship opportunities are an important part of our homeschool curriculum. For us, internships serve two purposes. One, it allows the child to engage with a wide demographic of people, while troubleshooting daily conflicts that one might find in a regular job environment. Two, it also enables the child to have opportunities where they can take a talent or hobby and have greater opportunity to experience it as a trade or viable business.

"Currently, our son interns one day a week for eight hours at the music studio where he takes lessons. He mirrors the studio manager during all of his jobs and activities, while also being given individual assignments with due dates that he works on throughout the year.

"We also do a lot of volunteer work, where the children are encouraged to step up and lead. Engaging in something beyond their personal desires provides greater understanding of what teamwork looks like in a business setting where task completion is linked to several moving factors.

"Both our daughter and son volunteer as counselors during the summer when many summer camps are available for younger kids. My son, who is fifteen, volunteers for multiple music camps as well as an art camp. My daughter, who is twelve, volunteers as a wrangler at an equestrian center, and she is responsible for the care and maintenance of horses as well as preparing them for riding. During the summer, she serves as a camp counselor; she's assigned a new rider and she helps them learn the ropes while also making them feel safe and keeping an eye on them to ensure their safety around the horses."

Extracurricular Activities

Many extracurricular activities, such as 4H or martial arts, offer their own group learning experiences. As an early elementary dance teacher, I offer show-and-tell times, discussion on a dance experience, and voting for a song choice. Students who do not go to traditional schools are able to have these types of experiences through dance classes like mine, or in other extracurricular activities such as clubs, internships, sports teams, church youth group events, volunteer service opportunities, and internships.

None of us wants our children to miss out on academic opportunities that may prepare them for college or future careers. One of the greatest things about homeschooling is the freedom we have to customize the academic rigor and experiences we want our children to have. We can prepare our children for an Ivy League school while homeschooling if that's what our family desires and what is important to the child. With a little research and creativity, we can provide our children with classroom experiences outside of traditional schools. Our homeschooled children do not need to miss out on academics.

Can-Do Assessment to Optimize Academics

❑ I have the means to purchase or borrow math, science, history, and literacy curriculum.

❑ I can research online (via web browser and social media) independent study programs, homeschool-charter schools, enrichment centers, and other interest-based programs for my area.

❑ I have transportation for my child to and from in-person opportunities.

❑ I can own, borrow, or rent a computer, or spend time at a computer lab at a local library, for my child to utilize online opportunities like Khan Academy or Outschool.

❑ I have time and energy to explore opportunities for advanced academic course work.

Chapter 12

What Will I Miss Out on If I Homeschool?

MANDI

That's right. This concern is all about you. What about *your* needs and wants? What will you potentially miss out on because your child is homeschooling? First we take an honest look at some of the possible ways you might miss out, and then we give ideas for minimizing or mitigating those potential losses.

What about My Career?

Homeschooling is quite a juggling act on its own, and making time for your own career can be difficult. We're not going to sugarcoat this—it can feel impossible at times. But we believe it can be done. Consider our personal examples. We homeschool, host a podcast, write a blog, run a cooperative group as coleaders, and here we are writing a book about homeschooling! Jessica also professionally teaches dance lessons for two different schools of dance for fifteen to twenty hours per week, with a kindergartner in tow. It's hard but possible, and a support network makes all the difference. For an in-depth look at managing work and homeschooling, see chapter 19.

What about My Interests?

It's good for our children to catch us reading a book, playing dominos, exercising, practicing the saxophone, designing our scrapbook pages, or chilling with old sorority sisters. When we develop ourselves and nourish our own hearts and minds, we are better inspired and equipped to pour into our children's hearts and minds.

These are some individual ways we (and our spouses) develop our own interests:

- listening to podcasts and books
- sitting on the couch for quiet reading time while the kids play or read
- watching an online exercise program to exercise daily (my kids like to join in)
- practicing the guitar or banjo in the evening
- spreading out puzzle pieces and working on the puzzle with an invitation for anyone to join in
- listening to a music playlist while getting ready in the morning
- attending live performances of a local band or professional dance company
- playing video games after dinner
- taking continuing education courses online or in person to further develop a career or area of interest
- continuing a Duolingo streak for second language learning
- going out to dinner or traveling with adult friends

We can share our interests with our children and give them the opportunity to come alongside us on their own. It's fun for us to engage our interests with our children. Here are some ways we do that:

- bringing my children to the corner café to sit with me while we each read our own favorite book
- taking my sports-loving son to play pickleball with me and another mother and son who are friends of ours

- skiing locally with another family on weekdays when the slopes are mostly empty

- teaching my daughters to sew blankets and bags for their dolls during free time on a homeschool day

- planning creative themed events together on a Sunday afternoon

Being intentional and allocating time during your daily schedule can be the interest-building gift you need. Sharing your interests might actually become the most teachable moments you have together as your child matures and grows into adulthood.

No Regrets with a Hybrid Model

Raszell, homeschool parent of three children, teaches homeschool Jiu-Jitsu, California

This dad shared his journey about how he was able to keep his career and dive in as a homeschool parent. He turned his black belt Brazilian Jiu-Jitsu skills into an opportunity to work with homeschool kids.

He shared, "As an African American father and homeschool teacher, I can wholeheartedly recommend the homeschool experience my wife and I have had. We hesitated in the beginning, as we are both full-time working parents, but after touring the campus we chose [a public charter school with a campus children attend up to two days per week while homeschooling the rest of the time], we both knew it was what was best for our kids (and thought we couldn't mess them up too much in kindergarten). That decision was made six years ago, and we haven't regretted it for a second. It's been an amazing journey to be involved in what the kids are learning and experience both the joys and frustrations during their learning process.

"They are homeschooled three days a week and on campus two days a week. We can tailor our day around all the extracurricular activities our kids are involved in (musical theater, piano, gymnastics,

Cub Scouts, Jiu-Jitsu, and various sports). And oftentimes, we work ahead to allow for a 'fun-day Friday' where we take a field trip to learn what we can at the zoo, tide pools, museums, or the beach. The local trampoline park offers homeschool PE hours too, which encourages the kids to focus and get the schoolwork done so we can make it on time for two hours of jump time. I am a black belt in Jiu-Jitsu, and I started teaching a homeschool Brazilian Jiu-Jitsu class two days a week as an alternative for PE as well.

"We have had a great experience so far and love the community we have with other homeschool families."

What about "Me Time"?

This is for the parent who does not go to a paying job once the kids are sent off to traditional school each day—the parent who gets six to eight hours to run errands, do chores, tackle projects, or even enjoy a cup of coffee in relative peace and quiet. We see you. We feel you. So listen closely . . . If you choose to homeschool, you will lose some "me time." No question about it.

However, you will not lose *all* of it. Some of us meet our "me time" needs through scheduling it as part of the homeschool day. We share some of our hacks here to see if this might be a potential solution for you too.

Utilize Hours of Free-Play Time

Many homeschool parents plan multiple periods of time in the homeschool day when their children play independently; these periods are thirty minutes to a few hours. Providing space in your children's day for self-directed activity supports healthy development of their sensory and vestibular systems. Taking breaks filled with aimless or creative play also helps children focus better on schoolwork (Wedge 2014). Now, think of what those hours of free play every day can do for your "me time."

Fun Fact: The Vestibular System

The vestibular system acts as one of the senses, keeping the brain updated on where we are in space as we move our head, sit down, and even stand still. It uses the inner ear to help us maintain balance. Developing this system is an important daily activity for children and can include typical activities children already do, like spinning, swinging, rolling, hanging upside-down, and picking things up off the ground (Fitzgerald 2023). Who knew that tidying the house is actually great vestibular exercise!

Establish a Routine

When "me time" free time becomes all about cleaning, doing chores, and preparing food by yourself, you may not get the refreshment you need. You can involve your children not only to alleviate your load but also to teach them the value of contributing as family members and respecting your home.

One way some homeschoolers involve their children is to build simple household tasks into their everyday routine. You can create a morning routine that includes a ten-minute pick-up time after breakfast; even toddlers can assist in this task. You can alternate lunch preparation with an older child, so you aren't always doing the work. Plan another ten-minute pick-up time before dinner, and assign a dish helper to clean up after dinner. Involving your children can look any way you want, but including them and sharing some of the weight can make your "me time" more meaningful.

Some homeschoolers design their typical day around a regular one- to two-hour "quiet time." Sounds glorious, I know. And it is! Each child plays, journals, or reads calmly in their room or in a private space. Maybe the younger ones nap, and the older ones play solitaire. It may take some work to establish a routine, but this type of daily rhythm provides some consistent downtime.

I Need More "Me Time"

When we need more "me time" than our regular routine allows, we have to get creative. You can trade off time with another parent, a spouse, a friend, or a grandparent. You can set earlier bedtimes to have more time to yourself. There are many ways to carve out downtime, and it is possible to still get the amount you need as you adjust and adapt to having your children with you all day.

Someday—sooner than you think—you might love having your little buddies with you more than you value your "me time." We can't always anticipate the changes that may occur as our situations evolve and we adapt to them.

What about Growing My Friendships?

In traditional schools, parents have plenty of opportunities to make adult friends and create community with the families of their children's classmates. Between participation as "room parent," attending book fairs and open houses, volunteering at the jog-a-thon, cheering for our team at Friday night football games, arranging playdates, and chaperoning field trips and high school dances, a participating parent will have no shortage of community. Same goes for homeschooling, but friendships are formed in different ways.

That Wonderful Bond of Friendship

Raising children together in a community of people who help each other, carpool together, encourage one another, and delight in shared experiences can be a wonderful bond during the school years. Let's stop for a moment and think of places this kind of community forms. We've seen it happen with sports or dance families, kid-saturated neighborhoods, and faith-based groups or churches. These communities do not depend on whether one is traditionally schooled or homeschooled. As parents, we can find or create a community wherever we can form meaningful bonds.

Make Friends On-the-Go

If you decide to homeschool, you won't be friendless. Some of us homeschool parents have more friends than we know what to do with. Homeschool parents and other family members make friends through their enrichment lessons and field trips. When homeschooled children are not yet driving, parents or family members often accompany them on every field trip, every play date, and every learning experience; there is no shortage of time to form friendships with homeschool families of your own choosing. If you enroll in a homeschool charter school or private school that offers electives and extracurricular activities throughout the week, each one provides an opportunity to meet other parents or grandparents coming and going.

Making Friends through a Co-Op

Through our co-op, we have grown lasting bonds with our friends' parents, grandparents, aunts and uncles, and even their cousins. The far-reaching arm of friendship with homeschooling families is amazing, because homeschooling is often a family journey. Sometimes grandma, great-aunt, or older sister acts as the parent at meet-ups and excursions.

Every year, our Halloween costume party is hosted by a multi-generational household that, at one time, had four generations living under one roof. Our co-op group hosts a "Mom's Night Out" every few months to ensure we adults are developing our friendships. We have camping trips and parties for the whole family to ensure our spouses get to be part of our close-knit community as well.

Making Friends through Conferences

Recently we attended a homeschool conference and made new friends. It wasn't fleeting; we actually took pictures with them and put their names and phone numbers in our contacts.

We are bound to find people we want to befriend at large homeschool conferences. There we mix with homeschool parents and grandparents; prospective, new, and seasoned homeschoolers; and people of a variety of cultures, ethnicities, and socioeconomic statuses. As long as we are friendly and open to learn about others, we can forge new friendships. Conferences are a terrific opportunity to meet and be met by prospective new friends.

Forming Lifelong Friendships

Antonea, retired homeschool parent with eleven grandchildren

Antonea shared this with me: "In 1996 I pulled two of my sons from the public junior high to homeschool them. A year later my nephew came to live with us, giving me three teenage boys to homeschool. Luckily, I did so with the support of women already homeschooling. These women not only became my friends and encouragement, but also my mentors as I began homeschooling teenage boys. We spent time together planning events, organizing service projects, and chaperoning field trips and adventures. We camped together every Labor Day weekend for years, even after our children became adults. These women became my lifelong friends. I make sure we get together as a large group at least once a year so we can reminisce on the joys of homeschooling our children. We share the joys of being grandparents and watching our children navigate parenthood. We lean on each other through hard times that inevitably come as we age. Thanks to these friends and my amazing kids, homeschooling was one of the greatest times of my life."

Parenthood is not always easy. We've heard it said: "The days are long, but the years are short." Each of our children will be at home with us for about eighteen to twenty years, and though it often feels like an eternity, their childhood will fly by and soon they'll be moving out. After that, we will get all the time we need for whatever we want to develop, be it our careers or our personal interests.

But at the present, if you choose to homeschool, you can plan to make homeschooling the environment where you pursue yourself and build friendships that can last your lifetime, long after the kids have flown the coop.

You can make homeschooling one of your interests by seeing it as your hobby and your passion, and work to know it and love it. And then, maybe, when you are all done homeschooling, you will look back on that time and realize that homeschooling was indeed for you too—it was for your relationships and for the biggest passion in life: your children.

Can-Do Assessment to Find Opportunities to Serve My Needs

❑ I am or can get involved in a community outside of the traditional school in which I can pursue individual friendships.

❑ I have access to other homeschooling families who I want to connect with and possibly grow and build a community together.

❑ I can plan a specific number of hours for "me time" or to develop my passions.

❑ I know how many hours per week I need to devote to my job/career/hobby/ personal relationships to feel fulfilled.

❑ The hours planned for free time and child care support provide enough time for me to pursue my interests and/or career. If not, I can make changes.

Chapter 13

What Will We Miss Out on If We Don't Homeschool?

MANDI

When it comes to homeschooling, the fear of missing out—FOMO—works both ways. By *not* homeschooling, you may miss out on maximizing the precious time you have with your children, customizing their education, and observing every academic achievement—no matter how small. Homeschooling life creates your own community and experiences that are unique to your family and can bring rewards that might not be worth trading for traditional school perks.

The Gift of Time

Marcus, homeschool parent of three kids ages nine to thirteen

Marcus shared his delight in being able to join in on his children's homeschool experiences and adventures. He wrote, "I have a job where it happens to work well for me to keep earlier hours. I intentionally arrive at the office by 6:30 a.m., which allows me to be home by 3:15 p.m. on most days so I can join in the homeschool fun.

"I am thankful when I return home in time to join my wife and children as they explore Mesopotamian culture or are preparing for their egg drop experiment. I cherish the opportunity to tackle a chapter of Latin with them or share an imaginative adventure through a read-aloud session before it is time for the evening busyness of dinner preparation or a youth sporting event.

"Instead of checking my social media feed while waiting in the school pick-up line, I get to jump right into the action of the school day. In this way, homeschooling allows me to extend the post-work family time and be an active participant in the excitement of the school day. I consider it a positive gift of time in this fleeting stage of life."

What would you rather miss out on? You decide! This is why we love school choice. There are many wonderful options, and you need to choose the one that best fits your children, you, and your family. If you are hesitant about homeschooling because you have FOMO, make a pros and cons list before you decide.

We provide some items for you to consider with your family. Talk these over together, review your family goals or mission statement, and decide what makes the most sense to miss out on. Viewing your decision from both sides should tip the scales and alleviate your fear of missing out.

By Not Homeschooling, You May Miss Out on Freedom

When we homeschool, our schedule is our own in every way. We do not have to report to anyone. Our family plans can be our priority. Our children's interests can be the center of their education. We select the curriculum, we explore various cultures, and we choose our communities. We are free to do school on the road, only in the evenings, or in intervals (for example) of six weeks on and one week off. We are free to spontaneously take a Wednesday off to visit Grandma and homeschool on Saturday morning instead. Homeschooling is a daily clean slate that we make our own.

. . . .

Freedom for a Teen Golfer

Micah, a homeschooled teenager, loves practicing at the local golf course's free putting green. He often receives helpful (and free!) advice from the golf elders who delight in seeing the next generation on the green. Micah shared, "When we finish our schoolwork, I love how we can just head over and play golf whenever we want."

. . . .

By Not Homeschooling, You May Miss Out on Family Time

When we design our days around our priorities and teach our children time management when we homeschool, we have as much family time as we want. Nonacademic activities such as sports, performing arts, animal husbandry, and art lessons can all be enjoyed without taking away from family time.

We also get to have our evenings together. Homework is nonexistent for many homeschooling families, because schoolwork is completed during the homeschool day. Parents, let that sink in for a moment—no homework! Game nights, learning new skills together, vacations, and field trips can all happen anytime without the confines of school schedules.

An added bonus: when we homeschool more than one child, our children may form deeper bonds with each other by learning together and from one another.

Notable Homeschoolers

You may remember the 1997 hit song "MMMBop" by the band Hanson. The Hanson brothers, Isaac, Taylor, and Zac, were homeschooled. Their parents chose to homeschool their seven children to promote family togetherness and flexibility. The Hansons' father traveled often for work and homeschooling allowed the family to travel with him. The family was very musical and encouraged Isaac, Taylor, and Zac in their own musical pursuits. Homeschooling gave the boys time and togetherness to focus on their goals. Taylor Hanson and his wife, Natalie, now homeschool their children (Fobbs 2018).

By Not Homeschooling, You May Miss Out On a Community That Fits You

When time is on our side, we can engage in the communities that fit our children's need for passions, interests, and fun. Nature co-ops, STEM clubs, or service-oriented groups are just a few ways that children and families can develop groups of friends to help them all grow together and toward their goals. Many people end up loving the community they are provided through the local school, but imagine a community that you seek out or create based on criteria that fit your family or children's needs best. (For more about community, see chapter 9.)

By Not Homeschooling, You May Miss Out on an Individualized Education

Personalized learning is a growing need; educators realize it can address disengaged students and help close the achievement gap. Judy Hughey, associate professor of special education, counseling, and student affairs at Kansas State University, wrote:

The goal of personalized learning is to engage students in the process, building on their interests, aptitudes, and strengths, thus creating intrinsic motivation for achievement and success. Students feel empowered when involved in goal-setting and decision-making processes. One primary key to effective individualized personalized learning is sparking the innate curiosity of students through active engagement with their environment. (Hughey 2020, 1–2)

Schools are implementing approaches such as blended learning as they work toward personalized learning experiences for students. The ongoing efforts of schools to evolve with current research and try new approaches are a potential benefit to students.

However, even with such efforts, what traditional schools can offer is a far cry from the truly customizable education that is available to our children when we homeschool. There are fewer limits on what we can offer our children in content and experiences. Our activities do not have to be grade-, age-, or peer-group specific. Available teacher time, computer accessibility, or topic choice can all be adjusted based on our own children's strengths, specific development, and interests. If you want to challenge your history-loving teen with academic rigor, do it. Spend time studying your history curriculum and pursue its extension activities, read a long list of corresponding literature like the Great Books, add Latin study, and delight in philosophical discussions and debate together. With a potential one-to-one student-to-teacher ratio, we can celebrate any milestone, explore topics in depth, and treasure new experiences together as a family.

By Not Homeschooling, You May Miss Out on Specialization

Homeschooling allows time for children to specialize in an interest, skill, or talent. Some children are drawn to a particular interest at an early age and begin to dedicate more and more time to that interest as they grow. Balancing that interest, traditional school, family time, and rest becomes an increasing challenge as a child reaches middle school. Eventually, something has to give, and one or more areas will be sacrificed.

What if you didn't need to make a sacrifice? What if your children could find balance while continuing their passions for computer coding or swimming? Homeschooling can free up more time in the day to pursue passions. The amount of time the average homeschooler spends on academics ranges between one to four hours depending on age. That is much less than the typical 6.5 hours at traditional school, plus homework. The extra time in your child's day can be put toward a potential career.

In *Peak: Secrets from the New Science of Expertise*, Anders Ericsson shares a study he conducted on a group of professional ballet dancers to determine what role practice had in their achievements. He concluded that the dancers who practiced more had higher ranks, and all had achieved an average of at least ten thousand hours of practice by age twenty (Ericsson 2016). The gift of time to focus and practice can help your child achieve their ambitious goals.

A Holistic Homeschool Approach

Iliana, homeschool parent and full-time realtor, California

Iliana, homeschool parent of a first grader and a twelfth grader, shared this with Jessica: "In a world where I feel that conventional education systems often leave individual needs and preferences unmet, I found solace and empowerment in the realm of homeschooling. My decision to homeschool was rooted in a desire to provide my children with a personalized and enriched learning experience, tailored to their unique strengths, interests, and pace of learning.

"Homeschooling offered the flexibility and freedom to design a curriculum that aligned with each child's individual learning style, strengths, and areas for improvement. Tailoring lessons and activities to their interests encouraged a genuine love for learning, fostering a sense of curiosity and engagement that I had rarely seen in a traditional classroom setting.

"One of the main factors influencing my decision to homeschool was the opportunity to instill strong values and morals in my children within the safe and nurturing environment of our home. I wanted to ensure that their education encompassed not only academic growth but also character development, empathy, critical thinking, and problem-solving skills.

"Moreover, the personalized attention and one-on-one teaching allowed for a deeper connection with my children, promoting open communication and a strong sense of trust. Their academic progress became a collaborative effort, tailored to their strengths and weaknesses, enabling them to thrive academically and emotionally.

"Through our homeschooling journey, we were able to engage in experiential and real-world learning, incorporating field trips, community service, and interactive projects. This holistic approach broadened their horizons and helped them grasp complex concepts with a practical, hands-on perspective.

"Over time, my children's academic achievements and personal growth reinforced my conviction in the decision to homeschool. They developed a genuine passion for learning, built a strong foundation of knowledge, and grew into confident, self-motivated individuals prepared to navigate the complexities of the modern world.

"While the decision to homeschool was not without challenges, the positive outcomes have far outweighed any initial concerns. Witnessing my children thrive academically, socially, and emotionally within the homeschooling environment has reaffirmed that choosing this unconventional educational path was indeed the right decision for our family."

Many of us, especially with tweens and teens, play that casual (and sometimes gross) question game Would You Rather? with our kids; and that's what this is. Be aware that if you choose to homeschool, your FOMO may just become JOMO, the Joy of Missing Out.

Can-Do Checklist to Weigh My FOMO for Each Choice

- [ ] I can make a T-chart and brainstorm with my family two lists: what my child will miss out on if they don't attend a classroom-based school and what my child will miss out on if we don't homeschool.

- [ ] I can make a decision tree or mind map to diagram the various pathways available to my child and our family. This will help me predict future opportunities that may or may not be available to my child. (Note: Decision trees are more useful for yes or no options, and mind maps are more useful for multiple-decision options. Search online for "mind maps" for more information.)

Part III

The Big Ones

"It doesn't matter what you're trying to accomplish. It's all a matter of discipline."

—WILMA RUDOLPH

The most common, serious concerns about homeschooling are often the most overwhelming; we call these "The Big Ones." But with some routine, discipline, and support, you can accomplish your goals and help your children do the same. Whether it be socialization, college admission requirements, or your extended family's acceptance of the choices you make, in this section, we dive in and share research and our experiences to help ease your concerns.

135

Chapter 14

What about Socialization?

JESSICA

We know countless veteran homeschool parents who agree that the most common concern they hear from other people is, "What about socialization?" Sometimes the concern is phrased as, "How will you socialize your child?" or "I don't want my kids to be weird."

Socialization has a few different definitions, but we will focus on two of them, one simple and one more complex, to consider this common hesitation. If someone is truly worried about our children socializing with others, we can confidently say there is no need to be concerned for *any* family that regularly socializes with others—friends, extended family, community groups, and so on. Most homeschooling families do not stay isolated from others.

So why is socialization such a common concern?

It's because a myth exists: homeschoolers lack socialization. To understand this concern about socialization, let's dive into the complex definition and see if we can unearth what the *real* concern may be.

Defining Socialization

Socialization can refer to interacting socially with others. That's the simple definition. Many sociologists further explain it as the process of learning to act or behave in a way that society deems acceptable. This more complex explanation is helpful in understanding the importance of socialization. Socialization is critical to every child's development and integration into society. Children begin socialization shortly after birth and go through the most crucial period during early childhood (Barkan 2011).

Antisocial vs. Socially Awkward

Is it logical to think that homeschooled children might become antisocial because of a perceived lack of socialization? No. Let's review the terms (often a necessary step when discussing socialization). Clinical antisocial behavior is more than a lack of socialization and is a serious personality disorder that can arise in any context (Widiger and Gore 2016). The term *antisocial* is used incorrectly when applied to the context of homeschoolers and socialization.

Sometimes people are concerned that homeschoolers will be highly introverted. However, there are no measurable statistics showing extreme introversion is a result of homeschooling or showing introverts are more likely to be homeschooled.

We think what people may really be worried about is having a "socially awkward" child.

Social Skills, Social Norms, and Social Awkwardness

Socialization is the ongoing *process* through which we learn social skills and social norms approved by our society. This occurs on the macro level as we learn about the values, habits, and attitudes of our larger society, but it also occurs on the micro level within small groups such as teams, work environments, or peer groups.

Social Skills

We are going to make a few assumptions that you taught your child (1) to greet others as is culturally appropriate, (2) to say please and thank you, (3) to share, and (4) to take turns. These social skills are often taught by parents as a natural part of raising children and are reinforced and refined through experiences, observations, and interactions outside the home.

The list of generally accepted social skills commonly taught to children includes:

- respect personal space
- gauge when to use eye contact and do so appropriately
- share (when appropriate)
- listen actively to others
- follow directions
- use proper cooperation and inclusion in group settings
- control one's impulses
- use widely accepted manners at the table and when greeting and interacting with others
- maintain personal hygiene
- have a positive attitude in group situations

Individuals may learn and use these social skills yet still behave in ways that are not socially conventional.

Social Norms

Social norms are the unwritten rules of behavior that are accepted by a group or society. Socialization is how we learn these rules. Individuals have the choice to conform to social norms or not. While there are no standardized criteria for labeling someone "socially awkward," the term is typically applied to individuals who seem at odds with the social norms and conventions of their peer group. People who have developed social skills and understand social norms may still not fit in with their group. But that doesn't mean there isn't a group for them.

Where Socialization Occurs

With this understanding of socialization, we remind ourselves that our children have social interactions often:

- within the home among adults and siblings

- outside the home:
  - among extended family and friends
  - at school
  - in community groups such as playgroups, co-ops, support groups, houses of worship, interest-based groups
  - in activity groups such as sports, clubs, lessons
  - in the community at grocery stores, movie theaters, baseball games, parks, museums, service projects

As you can see from this list, it is nearly impossible to avoid social situations; school is just one of many places where socialization can happen.

Home Is Where the Heart Is

Three moms share the joys of schooling in their homes

Krista, homeschool parent of a young teen in Missouri, shared, "My thirteen-year-old has many friends that she's very close with, but her strongest influences and who she spends the most time with are right here in our home."

Laura, parent of two middle schoolers in Washington, was asked what she loves best about homeschooling. She told us, "The relationships! I started homeschooling our two daughters in sixth and seventh grade a year ago. We are closer, I am still the main influence on them, and we enjoy family time. We get the best of them rather than the tired grumpy kids at the end of a long day at their former brick-and-mortar school!"

Debbie, who is homeschooling two sons in Texas, one in seventh grade and one in twelfth grade, told us this, "My teens will tell you their favorite part of homeschooling is that they get to wake up at noon and do school in the evening. For me, the best part has been getting to *know* them. We will be discussing a school topic but get off-track in conversations. It's such a privilege to be witness to what they are thinking and when they 'get' something. Also, I love the random hugs throughout the day."

Homeschoolers' Social Successes

Researchers who have studied the socialization of homeschoolers have dispelled the socialization myth. The 2007 National Survey of Children's Health found that homeschooled children had mental, social, and emotional health comparable to their traditionally schooled peers. This study concluded that homeschooled children were at no greater risk for socialization problems (Montes 2015).

The Role of Free Play in Socialization

Since socialization is how children learn social norms, our children need adequate opportunities for social interaction. Most importantly, they need to be allowed to interact freely with others. Parents can step in when they feel it necessary to interfere for safety, skill-building, or support, but the important aspect is for children to be in environments where they can freely test their interpersonal skills with others. In *Free to Learn,* Peter Gray describes free play "as play in which the players themselves decide what and how to play and are free to modify the goals and rules as they go along" (Gray 2013, 7). Free play is an effective and important way for children to practice their social skills and values, particularly in mixed-age groups.

In order for free play to be successful (and fun!), the players must learn to compromise or cooperate; otherwise, the play will end, and with it the children's fun. Mixed-age groups have less competition and more cooperation toward shared goals among players. Through play, children learn that rules are agreed-upon conventions that can be altered to meet changing conditions. Free play is an important way children gain the ability to discern for themselves the rules they choose to abide by within society.

We're All a Little Weird

It's time to reconsider the long-held stereotype of the "weird homeschooled kid." This stereotype is a concern we hear often from non-homeschoolers and parents considering homeschooling. What makes homeschooled children any more likely to be weird than non-homeschoolers? What's wrong with being weird? What's wrong with being different? From which groups are we drawing our social norms—society at large or a peer group of middle schoolers? Do we want our children to conform to the social norms of other middle schoolers? Where does that leave us?

Perhaps there are people you consider socially awkward or weird. Surely you can name homeschoolers, public schoolers, and private schoolers alike. Everyone's definition of *weird* is different. And if *weird* means "unique," maybe it is a label we should embrace. Mandi told people, "I'd rather be weird than ordinary" when peers at her traditional school told her she was "weird" (and Mandi was never homeschooled). We should change our mindset and celebrate the fact that some people choose to be themselves unapologetically, even if that makes them uncool or weird to others.

By not conforming to the arbitrary social norms of a particular group, our children can find the group that supports them in being themselves. Individuals who refuse to conform to certain norms are often the ones who change societal conventions. Consider the shift in culture from making fun of "nerds" to celebrating their accomplishments and respecting their differences. "Nerds" are now largely accepted as successful, functional, contributing members of society, to a much greater degree than in the past.

If our children are able to use their social skills to capably interact within society and understand the social norms and customs of different societal groups, that is successful socialization. The goal is for our children to confidently be themselves.

Our Social Experiences

Most homeschoolers we know are quite socially active. Numerous homeschooling friends of ours have told us that on a regular basis people, even strangers, share their admiration (and surprise) for how adept their children are at interacting with adults. Often, this praise applies also to how well children are able to play with others much older and younger than themselves. Most of the social situations our kids enter include children of wide age ranges and many adults.

For example, when Mandi and I get our families together, the children (ages five to thirteen) alternate between playing together and breaking out into smaller groups based on interest. The same thing happens with the eighteen families in our co-op: our forty-five participating children, ages two to fourteen years old, interact regularly with minimal interference from the parents. Conflict arises, naturally, but is an opportunity for the children to learn and grow.

Preteen Loves Her Co-Op

Eleven-year-old Sofia shares this about her homeschool co-op: "I am super grateful for how well I get along with everyone in the group. When I went to a charter school [half-day enrichment program] once a week, I had my best friends and everyone else was background noise. In the co-op, I feel like I can sit down and have a good conversation with most of the people. I feel like every kid in the group could be my best friend if I wanted them to be. They are all great to be around. Also, there aren't any bullies. We all treat each other equally and like we're just a huge group of friends—not where you might have a dynamic duo and the rest are just kids you can ignore and be unfriendly to. Having such an open community is great. I even like hanging out with the boys—they are all as cool as the girls!"

What If I Have One Child?

Stephanie, homeschool parent of a teen, Colorado

Stephanie shared with us the joys and struggles with socialization when homeschooling one child. She wrote, "As far as schooling an only child, like any situation, it has its pros and cons. Certainly one-on-one time is wonderful. But on the flip side I've had to intentionally pull away so my son could become more independent, which is more natural when you have multiple children. Also, because he's my only child, I often feel like I homeschool in a vacuum. Meaning, sometimes I'm guessing if he's on target, if what he's producing is 'normal' for his age, with no one else to compare him to. And I don't mean compare as in compete, but just have a baseline.

"I intentionally found ways for him to be accountable to others outside of me. For example, he is in a day-long co-op on Fridays, and I'm not in class with him. He took a math class at his charter homeschool last year and excelled. And he did a thirty-week entrepreneur course through the chamber of commerce. I look for things like that to help get us out of the 'vacuum.' He's also in a Spanish immersion class this year and sometimes a buddy from his co-op will come over, and they'll school together. Those all help.

"Socially, homeschooling an only child had some unique challenges and blessings. My son is super extroverted and an adventurer. So finding homeschool groups to do activities with was important. Also, being able to afford his interests has been a blessing with an only child. (We've had several rough years and are coming out of another period of eight months of unemployment).

"We prayed from the time we had our son that God would surround him with lots of people and children and comrades. God has given him that in spades! He's been invited on camping trips, week-long camps in Colorado Springs, and long mountain biking adventures with other families."

Stephanie shared another challenge: At first, she experienced "little stings" from large homeschooling families in the small, tight-knit town she had moved to when she started homeschooling. She said that homeschooling families frequently expressed surprise when they found out that she had "only one child."

Stephanie pushed through the hurt, and shared this: "So part of it was breaking into a community that was already established, which is always challenging to do. Most of these homeschooling families grew up here and grew up together, go to church together, etc. So I was an outsider on many levels and not just having an only child. Having lived in a town of 1,200 people, as well as big cities like San Diego and Denver, I feel like I was wise enough and have moved around enough to understand these people weren't intentionally being mean. They were just ignorant to the unknown (me), and relationship-building takes time. Time allowed us to show them differently, and I'm friends with some of the 'offenders' today."

Socialization should not be a concern that makes you hesitate to homeschool your child. You are a social being, and with your own tools, experiences, community, and additional enrichment, you can teach your child to stand kindly and unapologetically in society with confidence.

Can-Do Assessment to Help with Socialization

- ❏ I can continue the process of teaching my child social skills.
- ❏ I can provide my child with opportunities to socialize with different groups.
- ❏ I can make space for my child to play freely with others on a weekly basis, whether it be at public playgrounds, parks, or other public or private places.
- ❏ I can look past the "weird homeschooled kid" stereotype to let my child become who they are with confidence.

Chapter 15

Will My Child Fall Behind?

MANDI

Many prospective homeschoolers worry about their child falling behind. It does happen sometimes; your child may "fall behind." Of course, this is a concern of educators in the public school system as well. There are a few things to consider when diving into this concern as a prospective homeschooler. First, what criteria is used to determine "behind"? Second, what are some reasons children fall behind? Third, how can you prevent or remedy falling behind?

What Criteria Are Used to Determine "Behind"?

"Falling behind" typically refers to a student not progressing or achieving at the same level as their peers or the expected standards for their grade or age group. Many of us, since we were kindergartners, have been trained to think that grades and test scores are the ultimate measurement of student achievement and progress. State standards (and associated high-stakes tests) are an important part of the public-school program, and not meeting the standards, or "falling behind," is a nationwide concern.

Standards are the goals for student achievement, specified for each grade level and subject (math, reading, science, history, and others). They are typically developed by state governments. Your state's department of education creates its own list of these goals, which are used by teachers in traditional public schools (GreatSchools 2023). These standards ensure that teachers are focused on the same learning goals. There are also national standards known as Common Core. State leaders established work groups to develop these standards, which are voluntary for states to adopt (Council of Chief State School Officers, n.d.).

State standardized testing uses the same or similar questions for each student, scored the same way, in order to measure student achievement across the state for each grade level.

When Standards and Standardized Tests Matter

Standards can be a helpful tool in ensuring children are ready for the next learning level, be it from middle school to high school or high school to college, but do they matter in the home school environment before college? If you plan on homeschooling for a short period of time, let's say one to two years, then yes, state standards and test scores will matter. Reentry into the public traditional school may require that you stay on schedule with the grade-level scope and sequence. Also, upon reentry, students may be tested for placement in class reading groups and math groups, and for accelerated programs.

When Standards and Standardized Tests Do Not Matter

If you decide to homeschool for a longer or indefinite period of time, the state standards' grade-level scope and sequence don't really matter. Let's say, instead of learning geography this term like traditional students in the same grade, your homeschooled student develops an interest in and pursues a deep study in Asian American history. A standardized test may only measure the understanding of geography for the term, which would not reflect what your child has actually learned. This may mean that your child will be labeled as "behind" in state standards, but, in reality, your child is outside of, or beyond, the state standards and tests and not bound to the state's schedule. You are free to pursue developmentally appropriate, interest-led, and unique learning experiences and activities that suit your individual child.

Other Ways of Falling Behind

Falling behind can still be a concern when homeschooling. There are multiple ways that our children can "fall behind," whether it's in the amount of schooling hours, the curriculum we choose, or when compared to other children. The bottom line is that we need to keep in mind that every person's educational journey is unique to them.

Falling Behind on School Hours

The traditional school provides on average one thousand hours of schooling per year (National Center for Education Statistics 2020). This may seem formidable to keep up with at home, but when homeschooling, we don't need to log one thousand hours of school-related activities. A 2015 study of second-graders and fifth-graders showed that elementary school academics are taught for two to three hours per school day (Rosenshine 2015). This adds up to about 360–520 hours per year. During the rest of the school hours, students are engaged in art, music, physical education, and so on—probably what your child is already doing outside of traditional school. If the number of hours matters to you (or is set by your state), just remember that your child is always learning, and most engaged experiences and activities can count as learning time.

Some states do require you to log a minimum number of hours or attendance. Be sure to check your state's requirements, which you can find easily at the Home School Legal Defense Association website (hslda.org).

Falling Behind the Curriculum Schedule

Homeschoolers have many options with curriculum schedules. Even though we can utilize our school district's year-long independent study program or purchase a full-year boxed curriculum, keeping on schedule with these types of curriculum can be stressful. Falling behind does happen, so we need to consider this in our decision-making process.

Before deciding to homeschool, it may be helpful to figure out what type of curriculum schedule you would feel most comfortable with as you gauge if this is a lifestyle you want. If your first option seems too difficult to keep up with, you can change your approach and try a different type of homeschooling curriculum. Many homeschoolers take an eclectic approach, choosing curriculum for each subject from different publishers to create a customized plan that fits their family's needs and schedule. Homeschoolers can also adjust the daily schedule as needed to support optimal learning.

For example, we can observe our children to see when they are most engaged, and then we can be flexible based on their natural rhythms. My older children sometimes choose to work on the next day's independent assignments for an hour in bed using flashlights, if it means they can stay up an extra hour and not have any independent work the next morning.

Mistakes We Made

Jessica

Don't write in pen! I love planners, organizing, and making checklists to help me plan our homeschooling life. I began my homeschooling journey by looking at the curriculum, making lesson plans, and scheduling our weekly work for the whole school year. What I learned is that life doesn't always go as planned.

Seeing my plan in pen on paper made me feel like I was constantly falling behind. The reality was that we merely postponed items in the planner for spontaneous learning experiences. I had to give myself permission for my plan to change without the feeling of failure.

 Eventually, I learned a few things: (1) Write lesson plans in pencil; (2) Write lesson plans separate from my planner, without dates, and check them off when done; and (3) Record the schoolwork we completed each day into my planner in order to keep track of where we left off and what we accomplished (sometimes referred to as "reverse planning").

Falling Behind Other Children

Have you ever said something like, "Your child is learning decimals *already*? Mine just started subtraction!" In our competitive culture, it is hard not to compare another child's mapping skills with your own child's lackluster attempts at drawing the four cardinal directions. To be direct: stop it. Stop comparing your child's achievement with other children's. Instead, consider and celebrate your children's own unique strengths and accomplishments.

Increased Confidence

Mai, homeschool parent, California

Mai, mother of three, whose children were in traditional school for most of their elementary years, shared that their confidence improved significantly after being homeschooled, and now they can work at their own pace without the anxiety of not performing as well as their peers.

 "My children suffer from varying degrees of anxiety. Homeschooling takes out the stress of feeling like they are competing against a class of twenty-five to thirty-five students or an entire grade level. At home, when they do their work, I don't emphasize that they need to get an A. In fact, I only flag work that is not passing, which is below a C. This information tells me if they did not fully understand the lesson, so we know if we need to go back to spend more time on the lesson. This process takes out the stress and competitiveness they don't want so they can thrive in this stage in their lives and may pursue a competitive side later, if and when they're ready, no pressure."

How Can You Prevent or Remedy Falling Behind?

If you are concerned about falling behind state standards by homeschooling, then our advice is to adhere to them by either using curriculum that meets state standards (many label the standards they address) or using another type of curriculum and keeping track of state standards independently. If your child has fallen behind in traditional schooling, homeschooling can give your child more time and one-on-one attention to get caught up. We want to caution you, though, that state standards can be rigorous and most students may fall behind at one point or another. The truth is, a standards-based education isn't the best fit for every student. Developing your homeschool mission statement and making a list of priorities before starting helps you identify your goals for homeschooling.

Develop Your Homeschool Mission

Taking on your children's education and bringing it in-house can be intimidating. Once you make a decision to homeschool, one of the best things you can do is develop a mission statement. A unique mission statement about why you want to homeschool and what you want for your children and your family in this adventure helps you establish your priorities. Periodically reviewing your mission statement can realign your focus and help you gain perspective on your children's progress, whatever it may be.

Educational Gaps

The world is full of interesting ideas and beautiful topics, and there is no way all of them can be learned by our children by the time they fly the coop. Whether children go to public school, private school, or home school, there will be content left uncovered. There will absolutely be educational gaps. The best news? As homeschool parents, we get to decide what those gaps will be.

While the trek of a homeschooled student may look different than that of a traditionally schooled student, there are multiple paths to a good education. "Falling behind" can be a matter of adjusting our perspective and appreciating what our children excel at and enjoy.

Can-Do Checklist to Ensure My Child Does Not Fall Behind

❏ I can access my state's standards.

❏ If it's important to me, I can find a curriculum that meets state standards.

❏ I can observe my child and name some of my child's strengths and areas that they excel at naturally or in which they show great interest.

❏ I can identify the concerns I have about falling behind (classroom hours, curriculum schedule, other children's progress, state standards, testing scores) and make a plan to address them.

❏ I can develop my purpose for homeschooling and use it to reorient my perspective and adjust my educational plan as needed.

Chapter 16

What about College?

JESSICA

All children, regardless of whether they attend traditional school or home school, will have their own unique goals for entering adulthood. While the question starts with, "What will my child do after high school?", the actual concern we hear most often is, "Can a homeschooled high school graduate get admitted to a four-year college or university?" Maybe your child is determined to go to a specific university, or maybe your child is unsure about college but wants to be prepared to apply, just in case. Either way, we want to assure you that homeschooled students have every opportunity to get into their college of choice, and you can help them do it.

✓ Notable Homeschooler

In 2023, Josiah Meadows, a homeschooled student, made headlines for delivering the Latin Salutatory at the Harvard University commencement. He was homeschooled by his parents using an eclectic mix of curriculum, tutors, online enrichment, and standardized tests. He graduated from Harvard with a B.A. in government, Secondary in economics, and Language Citation in Latin. His commencement speech can be watched online, but make sure you have the subtitles on—he delivers it in Latin!

Homeschooling Options for High School

As discussed previously, there are many educational support programs for homeschooling families. Families can continue to privately homeschool and manage the process of college admissions completely independently. Some families utilize private school umbrella programs that provide assistance with transcripts and diplomas while allowing them to privately homeschool their children. Many families choose to enroll in independent study programs (available at traditional public schools, public charter schools, or private schools). These programs may provide Advanced Placement (AP), honors, and International Baccalaureate (IB) courses, as well as award students with diplomas and transcripts.

Preparing for College While in High School

Just the same as traditionally schooled students, homeschooled students and their families plan and prepare for the possibility of college when starting high school. There are numerous ways to do that, and helpful tools are available.

Recordkeeping

An important aspect of preparing for college admissions is recordkeeping. The records will eventually be used to create a transcript (more on transcripts later). Recordkeeping can include work samples that are organized in a portfolio. Samples provide evidence of educational progress, academic achievements, presentations, science fair submissions, awards, published essays, reading logs, test scores, and enrichment activities, whether experienced in-person or completed online. Homeschoolers often have impressive records that compete well with their peers, no matter the school choice.

Extracurriculars

While in high school, many students participate in *extracurriculars*—that is, activities in addition to credit-earning academic subjects. Parents considering homeschool for their high schoolers can check online for the entrance requirements and recommendations from their child's list of preferred colleges. Extracurriculars include sports, clubs, hobbies, and other activities that contribute to a student's holistic development. Extracurriculars not only put students' passions to use, they are opportunities for students to shine.

Life-Enhancing Activities

Beyond grades and GPAs, colleges don't always look for the same things, but instead differ in the values they place on various character traits, perspectives, and extracurricular participation. Homeschoolers tend to have the flexibility to focus on developing depth in life-enhancing activities of their choice. Here are a few ways for homeschoolers to prepare for college:

- Volunteer for an organization of interest and spend quality time there.
- Try entrepreneurship and build a micro business.
- Participate in apprenticeship or shadowing opportunities.
- Develop talents such as playing a musical instrument, acting, graphic design, or robotics.
- Travel to take a course or volunteer in another country to learn history, experience new cultures, and gain new perspectives. (BestColleges 2023; Campbell 2018; CollegeData, n.d.)

Do any of these life-enhancing activities sound like an endeavor your child would be excited about? Homeschooling could allow your child to devote the time needed to grow and excel in something that not only affects their college applications, but also changes their life.

Passion Service Projects

Service hours prepare us for a life of awareness and compassion toward others. While clocking volunteer hours at an established charity is valuable for any college hopeful, undergraduate colleges may be more dazzled by time spent creating or building a service project from the ground up. We can help our teens take their passion and share it with others through service, whether or not we homeschool. But many homeschoolers appreciate the flexibility of a schedule that allows teens additional time to serve others during the school year.

Author Shellee Howard writes about this in *How to Send Your Student to College Without Losing Your Mind or Your Money*. She explains that students need to be able to answer questions such as "What is something about you that I cannot read in your application?" and "What makes you different from the tens of thousands of other kids applying to this college?" (Howard 2017). A passion project can be the answer!

The best part? Organizing an event or program that benefits people in local communities or around the world may be a life-changing experience. Passion put to good use can be very appealing to colleges.

Dual Enrollment

Many homeschoolers enjoy the benefit of dual enrollment. In most states, high school students can be enrolled concurrently at a community college, earning dual credit (credit for high school and college). With the availability of online classes, this can be an excellent option for homeschooled students. Not only will they receive a transcript from the college listing the courses they took, but they can also work toward college requirements (and possibly their future degree), saving both time and money. It's important to confirm that the credits are transferable to future colleges of choice, since not all colleges and universities maintain the same criteria and standards.

Standardized Testing

Homeschooled students can register to take AP and CLEP exams and ACT, SAT, and SAT subject tests to provide scores to prospective colleges and universities. These test scores can help address the concern that undergraduate schools *might* not recognize the homeschooler's transcript courses or course work as a legitimate description of a student's achievements.

AP Exams

Did you know students can take an AP exam without enrolling in an AP class? Passing an AP exam may require extensive rigorous study; however, your children can obtain the necessary course-of-study information and prepare for the exam on their own. To register for an exam as a homeschooler, pay the registration fee for each subject test and find a testing site through College Board's AP Services (College Board, n.d.).

CLEP Tests

Homeschooled high schoolers can take a College Level Examination Program (CLEP) exam for a pass/fail score. With a "pass" score, a student can potentially earn three units of college credit for each exam. There are thirty-four exams in five subject areas that each cost in the same range as an AP exam. In some states, eligible low-income families can get a CLEP exam subsidized by the department of education.

Currently, 2,900 colleges and universities will accept college credit earned from passing a CLEP exam. It's important to check the CLEP College Board website for the list of colleges who accept CLEP exams for college credits. Participating colleges vary on the amount of credits they allow (Claybourn 2023). The CLEP College Board website provides free and low-cost preparation resources and services for the exams. Just as with some of the other standardized tests, the credits might not be accepted by the college or university of the student's choosing; however, a passing score still shows proficiency in college-level material.

ACT and SAT Exams

If a homeschooled student doesn't have many formal courses on their transcript, they can consider taking the SAT subject tests to show proficiency. Some universities no longer consider ACT or SAT scores, so it is important to do your research on specific schools. For example, at the time of this writing, the University of California system will not consider these tests for admissions decisions or scholarship awards but may consider them for course placement after enrolling in the university (University of California, n.d.).

Requirements and recommendations can change frequently. As your children enter high school, you should research college and university requirements and processes, especially those for homeschooled students.

Applications and Admissions

Because the number of homeschooled students continues to grow through the years, undergraduate colleges and universities are prepared to receive applications from homeschooled students. For the most part, homeschooled students apply the same way other students do; however, contact the admissions office to ask if they have a unique application process for homeschooled students. Resources like topcollegeguru.com and exploresolutions.org offer college admissions counseling and support. You do not need to tackle this alone.

In a survey of college admissions officers, a Dartmouth officer said of homeschoolers, "The applications I have come across are outstanding. Homeschoolers have a distinct advantage because of the individualized instruction they have received" (Klicka 2007). According to the National Home Education Research Institute, "Homeschool students are increasingly being actively recruited by colleges" (NHERI 2023). Research and studies show that in the past two decades, homeschooled students are not in want of admissions opportunities. Application requirements vary, but homeschoolers can excel at college prerequisites and earn a high school diploma, develop a competitive transcript, obtain letters of recommendation, stand out by participating in extracurriculars, and receive scholarships.

Diplomas

A high school diploma is simply a certificate attesting that a student has completed the course of study required to graduate. Private schools set their own requirements and issue high school diplomas. Parents who homeschool their children privately can create diplomas for their children to attest to the completion of a secondary education (Accredited Schools Online 2023). Websites such as homeschool.com provide free diploma templates. If you prefer, you can order a professionally printed diploma with an attractive cover to be mailed to you from websites like homeschooldiploma.com.

Transcripts

Transcripts are lists of courses taken, with descriptions and associated grades where applicable. Colleges and universities understand that the transcripts of homeschooled applicants are unique. The key is for homeschoolers to provide as much detail as possible so an admissions department has an accurate understanding of the student's academic accomplishments.

This might seem overwhelming, but there are various resources to aid you in writing transcripts. One resource that we recommend is the Home School Legal Defense Association (HSLDA), which offers an inexpensive transcript-writing tool as well as a free transcript template on their website.

Letters of Recommendation

Letters of recommendation from adults outside the family are essential for homeschoolers. Students can have these letters written by coaches, teachers, counselors, mentors, workplace managers, and other adults who can speak to their skills, accomplishments, and character.

Sometimes people worry that homeschooled children will not interact with adults other than their parents or guardians. This has not been our experience. Numerous adults are involved in our children's lives and can authoritatively speak to their achievements and abilities, including (for example) a golf coach, a co-op leader, and a piano teacher.

Extracurriculars

Most high schoolers planning for college work diligently to have a strong list of extracurriculars, some of which we mentioned previously. Extracurriculars can be listed directly on a college application or discussed in a college essay. A unique set of extracurriculars can help a student stand out from the many applications an admissions department receives.

Scholarships

Many parents wonder if homeschooled students are eligible for college scholarships; the simple answer is yes. They may be ineligible for some scholarships, as their educational qualifications don't always check the same boxes as those of traditionally schooled students. However, there are scholarships awarded only to homeschooled students. In general, homeschooled students apply for scholarships in the same way as other students.

Jessica's Journey to College

My own unique journey as a homeschooler started in high school when I was fourteen years old. I enrolled in an independent study program through a local public charter school and chose to utilize the dual enrollment program at my local community college. Soon I learned from a college admissions counselor that I could graduate high school early, at age sixteen, with a basic diploma (fewer credits required). I could continue taking community college courses for another year, have enough units to transfer as a junior to a four-year university, and not have to take the SAT exams. My mom was hesitant about this fast track to college, but my maturity and the savings in time, money, and energy made it the obvious option.

So I did it! I transferred to the university as a junior at seventeen years old and earned my bachelor's degree just before my twentieth birthday. Throughout the process, I felt empowered because of the opportunity to make the decisions I thought were best for my future.

College Readiness and Success

Research in the past two decades establishes that homeschooled students can be well-prepared for and succeed in college. These studies found the following:

- Homeschooled students scored higher on standardized academic achievement tests compared to public school students (Ray 2004; Treleaven 2022).

- Homeschooled students were prepared for college and performed at least as well as traditionally schooled students (Ray 2011).

- Homeschooled students ended their freshman and senior years of college with higher GPAs than their traditionally schooled counterparts (Cogan 2010).

- Homeschooled students had a higher college graduation rate, 66.7 percent, than the overall population, 57.5 percent (Cogan 2010).

Rest easy about college admissions. While homeschooling parents and students may have to make extra effort to provide evidence of academic achievements and accomplishments, homeschooled students are just as prepared for college and perform at least as well as traditionally schooled students.

Can-Do Assessment for Preparing for College Admission

❑ I can look into various schooling options available for my child, including dual enrollment at a local community college.

❑ I can utilize the resources available to me to learn about high school diplomas, transcripts, testing, and scholarships.

❑ I can do some research or find a college admissions counselor to help me understand the college admissions process, especially requirements specific to homeschooled students.

❑ I can assist my child in finding extracurricular activities and community service opportunities.

❑ I recognize that there is not one specific way for students to get accepted to college and that homeschooling is not a disadvantage.

Chapter 17

Can I Homeschool My Neurodivergent or Gifted Learner?

MANDI

Sometimes educating our unique children requires a little (or a lot!) more from us than what we think we can give—be it special knowledge, remarkable patience, or artful finesse. Are we up to the task?

Worry and feelings of inadequacy might overwhelm and paralyze us, making us doubt ourselves. We ask, "Can I provide an effective educational environment outside of public school services?" "Can I do this without IEPs, 504 plans, and school-provided therapies?" This chapter is to help you know that it is possible— you can do this.

Many families experience numerous benefits by homeschooling their neurodivergent and gifted children and have expressed their gratitude for the homeschooling lifestyle and the progress, joy, and connection it brings them. We hope that with reassurance, research, and resources, these benefits can be a possibility for you too.

Homeschooling Helps with Dyslexia

Sarah, homeschool parent of a child with phonological processing deficit/dyslexia, California

We learned from Sarah that homeschooling part-time made a positive impact in her child's elementary school years. She shared, "I chose to homeschool before I knew my daughter was going to struggle in school and need an IEP, but it was a huge blessing to be able to go slower and tailor-fit lessons to meet her needs. I was also able to be involved firsthand in her education, and I think she would have been lost in a sea of other kids if we did not do what we did in the younger years especially.

"She was diagnosed with phonological processing deficit; in simpler terms, she has dyslexia. By using a hybrid elementary school that involved homeschooling her three days per week, we were able to slow down and cut out work that did not meet her needs. She is now in high school at the same hybrid school and is home one day per week. It is no longer homeschooling, but I am still very involved and making sure she is staying on track and her accommodations are being used in the classroom as needed. Using a charter school that included homeschooling was the perfect balance for our situation. We are thankful for the amazing support she was given and the way they celebrated her progress even if it was not the same as everyone else."

Children with Disabilities

Many families choose to homeschool their children with disabilities. In studies as far back as 2012, between 20 to 24 percent of homeschooled students had a disability (National Home Education Surveys Program, n.d.), which is comparable to the 22 percent of public schooled students that had a disability. Thus, the ratio of homeschooling families and traditional school families with children with disabilities is about the same. Also, 34 percent of homeschooling families state that their children's special needs or physical or mental health were an important reason for choosing to homeschool (McQuiggan and Megra 2017). So, if you choose to homeschool a child with a disability, you will not be alone.

Neurodivergent Children

Whether or not learning difficulties are disabilities is a subject of ongoing discussion, so we use the term "neurodivergent." *Neurodivergent* refers to "variation in the human brain regarding socialization preferences, learning, attention, mood, and other mental skills" (Morin and Kircher-Morris 2023, 47). It is a nonmedical umbrella term for people with struggles and strengths that include (and are not limited to) learning disabilities (LD), attention deficit/hyperactivity disorder (ADHD), autism spectrum disorder (ASD), and more (Cleveland Clinic 2022).

Twice-Exceptional Students

Twice-exceptional (2e) refers to children who are intellectually gifted and have one or more learning disabilities (Davidson Institute 2021a). This distinct group of children was first identified in 1977. Experts estimate that 2 to 5 percent of the gifted population have LDs, and 2 to 5 percent of students with LDs are gifted (Bracamonte 2010).

Check with an Expert

In this chapter, we share important research, statistics, and resources from those who have lived a homeschooling life with neurodivergent children; however, we are not experts in this field. The Learning Disabilities Association of America recommends that you seek guidance from a professional—such as a clinical psychologist, neuropsychologist, learning disabilities specialist, or others—for your child's educational path. We hope this chapter will help lead you toward making the best decision for your family.

What Does Gifted Mean?

Gifted children are most commonly identified as those who outperform their peers in one or more academic areas (Davidson Institute 2021b). It is estimated that about 20 percent of homeschooled students are gifted students who were dissatisfied with their traditional school education (Lee 2016). Homeschooling can be advantageous for gifted children by helping accelerate their learning and avoid unnecessary repetition. Parents should be aware of their child's gifted ability and encouraged to help their child progress and succeed with it. Your child can be assessed by a trained professional (you can ask your pediatrician for a reference) using tests in combination with observations (by parents, teachers, friends, and so on) and work samples over time. If your child is gifted, check out the National Association for Gifted Children (NAGC), an organization providing support to parents and educators of gifted students.

As awareness about 2e children grows, the essential need to customize our children's education grows too. It is reassuring to have options like homeschooling to help our unique children excel.

Why Choose to Homeschool?

Why do parents choose homeschooling for their neurodivergent or gifted children?

- Some parents want to allow their child the space, time, and environment to develop and learn without restrictions and at an individualized pace. They want time to explore, find, and use the best tools to meet their children's needs.

- Due to their unique needs or gifts, some children experience judgment from teachers or other students. I know from my teaching experience the potential trickle-down effect of this judgment, or freedom from it, and have seen it impact children's self-confidence and emotional well-being on multiple occasions.

- Some parents feel that the traditional schools don't serve neurodivergent and gifted students as fully as their child needs due to a lack of training, resources, or services. These parents may have better access to support outside of the traditional school.

- Some parents want the challenge of learning additional skills and tools to support their child. While it might be difficult at first, learning how to engage and educate their child helps equip parents with tools for their entire lives together.

- Some parents wish to avoid having their child labeled. (This is an area of disagreement among homeschoolers; others support early assessment since it leads to early intervention for learning disabilities [Coalition for Responsible Home Education 2021].)

These parents recognize that homeschooling not only customizes the learning experience, but also plays a major role in developing their child's whole self.

No Labels Are Needed

Some parents are worried about labeling their child with a diagnosis. Sarah (from the previous story), who has a child with dyslexia, advises, "Just because they have a diagnosis doesn't mean it needs to be their label or that others even need to be made aware of the label. Protecting your child is most important, and you have the most control when you are homeschooling."

Keeping Your Own Pace

Sara, homeschool parent of three teenagers, including one with developmental delays, California

Sara adopted her son when he was four years old. He had severe developmental delays from being kept in a crib for his first four years of life. Now he is a teenager. She shared, "With our son, his developmental delay meant that he would always be a grade level or two behind other children. Homeschooling him up to grade six was the best decision we ever made because there was no pressure to conform, he could develop at his own pace and in his own way, and we were able to keep his confidence intact.

"Judgment was our greatest fear. Sometimes it isn't even the judgment of others, but the neurodivergent student becoming discouraged that they cannot function in certain ways at the same level as their peers. Some peer pressure can be healthy, but if there is an underlying condition preventing a child from performing at grade level, their own observations about their own performance (comparing themselves with peers) can be hard to process emotionally and may harm their self-esteem."

Benefits of Homeschooling

By homeschooling, and receiving services if needed, we can provide our children with truly individualized learning and a supportive environment.

Benefits for Neurodivergent Children

Brittany Gonzalez is a special education expert and homeschool parent to neurodivergent children. She shares her thoughts on the benefits of homeschooling for neurodivergent students in her 2023 article, "30 Benefits of a Neurodiversity-Affirming Home Education (NDAHE)."

These benefits include the *reduction* of the following:

- bullying
- negative peer influences
- sensory overload
- anxiety
- pressure to conform (academically and socially)
- distractions, interruptions, and transitions
- time spent on busywork
- negative school culture or politics

Additional benefits of homeschooling include *increases* in the following:

- positive social interactions with family and friends
- creative hands-on and experiential learning
- time and schedule flexibility for interventions and therapy
- time in pursuit of interests or hobbies
- parental involvement
- physical activity (Gonzalez 2023)

A common thread here is that homeschooling can help children live and learn in a less stressful environment. Being pulled out of class for therapy or singled out by a teacher for unique qualities can be a source of shame and embarrassment for some children. It's hard for children to focus and learn when they feel stressed and unsafe (Stixrud and Johnson 2019). If you need to create a safe space for your children with their unique gifts, abilities, and challenges, homeschooling can be the way to do that.

Benefits for Gifted Children

There are numerous ways to offer gifted students the opportunities they need to thrive, and homeschooling is one of them. Even if your child's ability surpasses your own, it doesn't mean you cannot teach your gifted or twice-exceptional child. You can! In fact, experienced parents share that there are many benefits to homeschooling your gifted or 2e child.

Benefits include the *reduction* of the following:

- waiting for others to finish tasks and bookwork
- busywork
- sensory overload
- ridicule
- requirements for children to sit still for longer than they are able

Benefits also include *increases* in the following:

- meeting children where they are, with their unique gifts and struggles, and tailoring learning to their needs and interests
- learning that goes beyond the limits of assigned grade levels or school-day schedules
- children choosing resources (curriculum, books, classes, activities) that serve their interests and preferred learning styles
- children's freedom to explore their creativity
- opportunities for relationships with other families and children who share similar gifts and interests (through clubs, interest-led activities, and co-ops)
- time to spend with children teaching necessary life skills (Kessler 2021; West 2023)

If gifted or 2e students feel like they are moving at a snail's pace for some subjects within traditional schooling constraints, homeschooling can be the very thing that releases them to explore their rabbit trails of curiosity.

Potential Challenges

Before making any decision, it's important to know the challenges you may face. Screening, diagnostics, and services should be available to all children, including homeschoolers. Under the Individuals with Disabilities Education Act, public schools are required to offer free evaluations to *all* children with possible disabilities. However, the requirement that public schools provide services to homeschooled children is not enforced. The level of services available to

The Power of a Loving Parent

Nicole, owner/teacher at a homeschool enrichment center, former homeschool parent, California

Nicole (pseudonym) shared her experience parenting a child with autism spectrum disorder. "Experienced homeschoolers will tell you that homeschooled children do not miss out on social opportunities. It is true, but for my oldest child, social situations were particularly difficult. My oldest child is on the autism spectrum. She grew up being misunderstood and treated poorly. People thought she was mean and dumb. She desperately wanted friends, but nobody wanted to be around her. Not kids. Not adults.

"While we did start out homeschooling, there was a year and a half when I took a full-time job, and I put my two older kids in school. My oldest was treated very poorly in school. Instead of recognizing her needs and providing caring solutions, her teacher blamed her bad behavior on homeschooling. My daughter was insulted in class and ignored at recess. As an adult, my daughter admitted to me that at the tender age of seven, that year in school was the first time she felt suicidal.

"Looking back at our homeschooling years now, I was certainly far from the perfect, caring mom that my daughter needed. But I always loved her, and I did what I could to provide for her in the best way I could—and I still do. While my daughter was able to graduate from college, she will never be 'normal.' She is still my child who struggles with life and friends. But what would have happened if I had not brought her back home after her foray into public school? It is unimaginable. I am honored to be a constant in her life and to be there for her when the rest of the world wants to fire her, cancel her, evict her, and never deal with her again.

"All the degrees in the world will never compare to the power of a loving parent. Better than anyone, we know what our children need and we're in the best position to provide it to them. You are your child's best friend and advocate. You do what you need to do for your children without waiting for permission from the school system."

homeschooled students with disabilities varies by state and county, often making it necessary for parents to advocate for their children and their rights for services under the Americans with Disabilities Act (Coalition for Responsible Home Education, n.d.).

For an alternative to public school services or other state programs, there are organizations like The Nectar Group, Raising Lifelong Learners, Homeschooling with Dyslexia, and Learning Disabilities Association of America that are able to assess and provide cognitive training, homeschool support (such as parent homeschool coaching), or other services and resources.

Sara, mentioned earlier, also shared this: "I naively assumed in the beginning that I could do it all—teach a special needs child and homeschool two other gifted children. It was too much. However I was not ready to give up on homeschooling altogether. Instead I began collecting resources in the forms of tutors, educational aids, online supplemental education platforms, online tutors and teachers, etc., to help ease the tremendous pressure of managing the needs of three very different children at one time. Just because you choose to homeschool doesn't mean you have to do everything yourself. I even enlisted the help of a tutoring company from time to time to help with math and language arts when I was getting stretched thin."

Tools for Homeschooling

Intentionally focused activities and daily practice at home can help you and your child celebrate every bit of progress and take comfort during the frustrating and difficult parts of homeschooling. There are many tools available that may resonate with you and help you see that you can do this.

Assessment

Interventions are based on assessments. Homeschoolers can access these assessments by visiting a medical provider, using the services public schools are legally required to offer, meeting with a licensed psychologist or other professional, or finding an online guide or curriculum that provides an informal assessment. Assessments may lead to referrals to educational specialists. Assessments also help us—often simply knowing more about our children's struggles can assist us in making more informed decisions, including determining the best schooling fit.

Curriculum as an Educational Tool

There are homeschool curriculums designed for specific diagnoses or giftedness. These can aid you in creating an optimal learning environment, with appropriate content, rigor, and pacing for your child. Curriculum that focuses on multisensory learning (visual, tactile, auditory, and kinesthetic) provides opportunities for students to rely more heavily on specific senses to meet some of their learning needs. Creative ideas for building the brain's ability to change (neuroplasticity) are built into some curriculums for students with specific learning challenges.

The Good Sensory Learning website offers free activity ideas, as well as curriculum you can buy, to focus on specific skills. There are homeschool curriculums that use the Orton-Gillingham approach, such as *All about Reading*, *Logic of English*, and *Barton*. Some families with neurodivergent children (whether homeschooling or not) have found this approach to be effective.

Games and Challenges That Make a Difference

Games are a creative, positive way to motivate and engage neurodivergent children. A benefit of homeschooling is that there is plenty of time to play games. What we love about games, besides the fun we enjoy together, is that once we learn a game, we can just play. We do not have to spend much time, if any, preparing for the lesson, because the lesson is built into the game.

Playing games such as *Taboo*, *Scattergories*, *Operation*, and Stacking Cups to improve processing speed and attention can add magic to your week. Other activities like one-minute recall, *Last Letter*, and reading to the beat of a metronome can assist in memory, focus, attention, and other cognitive skills (The Nectar Group 2023). Research and learn what skill-building games bring delight to your children and homelife; you can test them out now to build confidence in yourself as a guide and also to see if they are a potential avenue for your child if you decide to homeschool.

Autonomy

We know, this book is packed with accolades about the gifts of autonomy and free time, but they are all true! Autonomy is one of the major aspects we love about homeschooling. In *The Self-Driven Child*, neuropsychologist William Stixrud and his co-author, Ned Johnson, explain, "Throughout our decades of work we have seen that when children with ADHD, dyslexia, or other learning difficulties are given all the information necessary to make a decision and don't feel forced, they are extremely capable of choosing thoughtfully." They continue to say, "We have both seen for years . . . that when kids with special needs have a sense of control over their lives, they thrive" (Stixrud and Johnson 2019, 242).

Parent Development

Do you like learning? If you choose to be a homeschool parent, you may need to equip yourself with a toolbox of strategies, fun ideas, and connecting experiences to meet your unique child's needs. It might not be as hard as you think to find the help you require. You can expand your repertoire of knowledge and tools through websites, webinars, social media, courses on specific approaches, books, and conferences.

- The Homeschooling with Dyslexia website was started by a mother who homeschooled seven children with dyslexia, and it provides book recommendations, courses, and mentoring.

- The Yale Center for Dyslexia and Creativity recommends Sally Shaywitz's book, *Overcoming Dyslexia*, which includes a home program for parents to implement, among other tools.

- The Nectar Group offers free webinars for parents on different neurodivergent diagnoses, teaching important concepts (such as neuroplasticity) in an accessible style.

- Consider learning about the Orton-Gillingham approach (multisensory learning) and taking a course or two for educators and parents.

- The Davidson Institute offers support and information for gifted and twice-exceptional children, providing a community and resources for these unique students.

- There are multiple homeschooling resources and support groups on Facebook that you can join to gain insight, encouragement, and ideas from other homeschoolers with neurodivergent children.

- Explore SPEDHomeschool.com for online resources helping families with diverse learners reach their potential.

- Homeschool conferences provide opportunities to talk with professionals and specialists to explore the resources and assistance they provide to homeschooling families (curriculum, testing, tutoring, parent development, and more). At one conference, I spoke with a reading specialist and licensed school psychologist for about half an hour, one-on-one, about one of my children's reading difficulties. Her advice was pivotal in how I viewed my child's reading struggles. The only cost was the ticket to the conference and making time to learn from others.

In homeschooling, instead of forcing interventions upon our children without their consent, we get to invite them to choose how to work on a skill or physical activity with us. We can be that safe place as we help our children build their self-confidence and identity.

Can-Do Assessment to Homeschool My Neurodivergent, Gifted, or 2e Child

- ❏ I can obtain or have a diagnosis for my child, or I have the ability to have my child assessed either in-person or with curriculum-provided testing.

- ❏ If needed, I will be able to inquire further to find where professional services are performed and take my child to receive those services.

- ❏ I can lead my child in recommended exercises and interventions myself, or another support person can help with this.

- ❏ I feel comfortable trying different settings or environments for my child in order to find and provide their ideal learning environment.

- ❏ I can find a support network in person or online to help me understand and educate my child, knowing their unique needs.

Chapter 18

What about the Naysayers?

JESSICA

Not everyone agrees with homeschooling as a valid school choice. Some are against it completely. Others have a background or history that makes them feel negative about homeschooling, or it's too unconventional for their personal comfort. And there are some people who choose to be negative about things they don't understand.

Unfortunately, there may be people in our lives, whose opinions we value, who do not support our desire to homeschool our children. Whether it's a spouse, co-parent, grandparent, or sibling who disagrees, disapproval from the ones we love can make even the most determined parent question whether they are making the right decision for their children.

However, we won't know the full impact of our decisions until our children are grown. Even then, we still may not know. This applies to many of our parenting decisions, from whether or not to breastfeed a baby to the amount of screen time we allow our teens. What we can do is learn, research, ask questions, and then be confident in our decisions once they are made (and be willing to change if they are not successful).

How to Address the Important People

If your spouse, partner, co-parent, parent, or sibling doesn't support your desire to homeschool, we have a few suggestions about how to address them.

Understand the Concerns

A person's concerns feel valid to them based on their knowledge and frame of reference. Be a good listener. Ask questions to help them articulate their concerns. Listening to the concerns of someone important to you can help you understand how they feel. It also helps them feel heard and valued. Sometimes the fear of the unknown can cause concern, and once this is expressed and addressed, the person can move forward in a more supportive manner.

Share Research

Find meaningful ways to share information about homeschooling. Some people value scholarly articles that include research and data. A helpful place to start is the National Home Education Research Institute (NHERI), founded in 1990 by Dr. Brian D. Ray. Others value first-person experiences and success stories. There is an abundance of information available in all forms of media that supports homeschooling, provides statistics, and shares personal stories of students and parents.

Hand Them This Book

Do we address their concern in this book? Ask them to give us a chance to change their perspective. It's possible they need to be introduced to the greater world of homeschooling and hear this information from someone other than you.

Expose Them to the Lifestyle

The most important person or people who need to be on the same page as you are your spouse and any other co-parent. None of us wants to hurt our nuclear family relationships with our educational choices. The support of others is not as important, but your children's guardians do need to agree on the same educational model.

Propose a Compromise

We previously mentioned independent study options with public traditional and charter schools (offered in many states). Some of these schools have hybrid options where students are on campus a few days per week and homeschool the rest. Enrolling your child in one of these public school programs may ease the concerns of others while allowing you to homeschool.

Offer a Trial Period

The decision to homeschool doesn't have to be permanent. You can try it for a school year, a semester, or a summer and then reevaluate the decision. If you are able to pursue a trial period, we suggest going into it with the same gusto as if it were a long-term decision: make a homeschooling mission statement, find a support network, attend a conference, and research your curriculum options.

Can You Homeschool without Spousal/ Co-parent Support?

Yes. We've seen it done. Sometimes the spouse or co-parent comes around and supports homeschooling after seeing evidence that their child is doing well. Other times, they don't come around, and maintaining a happy home and successfully homeschooling children may not be possible. If a co-parent's mind cannot be changed, we can't say whether or not you should pursue homeschooling. Only you know the dynamics of that relationship. We realize how difficult it is to be in this position. Ultimately, if you are passionate about homeschooling, you will want your partner's support.

Naysayers around Town

Even if your loved ones fully support your decision to homeschool, you will likely encounter other people who disagree strongly. Here are our quick tips for dealing with those people:

- Determine whether discussing or debating with a naysayer is worth the effort.

- Find easy-to-repeat facts and research that support your decision. (For naysayers concerned about your child's socialization, share what you learned from chapter 14.)

- Provide a few homeschool success stories.

- Practice respectfully ending a conversation. You may mutually agree to disagree or need to remind a naysayer that you are the parent and the opinions of others are unlikely to change your mind.

- Give them this book. That's what we are here for. We want to be that voice for you. Hand it to your friend, dentist, or grandparent. If they truly care about the choices you make for your child, they will study the issue and not just insist they are right.

Nothing can be more challenging to our convictions than when someone we love and whose opinion we value disapproves of a choice that is important to us. At the end of the day, as the parents, we decide what is best for the well-being of our children, even if it means not having the support of those we love.

Can-Do Assessment to Navigate the Naysayers

❏ I can listen to and understand the concerns of someone who does not support me in homeschooling.

❏ I can find and share information in support of homeschooling.

❏ I can find a homeschool support network other than my spouse or loved ones if they don't support homeschooling.

Chapter 19

Is It Possible to Work and Homeschool?

JESSICA

Some of us have to, need to, or just really want to work . . . and yes, we can homeschool too. Working parents, including single parents, can homeschool successfully. It may require a major lifestyle change, but people do it.

Real Numbers on Working Families

In 2022, of the 33 million US families with children under the age of eighteen, 91.2 percent had at least one working parent (US Bureau of Labor Statistics 2023). Here is how this breaks down:

- Among married couples, 32.4 percent had only one parent employed.
- Among married couples, 65 percent had both parents employed.
- Of single-parent households maintained by fathers, 85.7 percent of fathers were employed.
- Of single-parent households maintained by mothers, 75 percent of mothers were employed.

It is clear that most parents have to work to support their families and households. Homeschooling families are no exception.

Working While Roadschooling

Sean, homeschool parent working full time

We met Sean, a single, full-time working homeschool dad, at a homeschool conference. He shared that in 2021, he hopped in his RV with his three children and roadschooled them most of that year's first semester while running his granite countertop business remotely. He said they traveled the country and lived their best lives.

Myths and More Real Numbers

Over the years we've homeschooled, we've heard many presumptions about the demographics of homeschooling families. Some have validity, but most do not. Here's why: the past decade of studies proved them untrue.

Myth: Homeschooling families must have higher incomes.

We have found that homeschooling families tend to make financial sacrifices in order to homeschool. According to the National Household Education Surveys Program of 2016, homeschool families make up the lowest percentage of families in the highest income bracket compared to public and private school families (McQuiggan and Megra 2017; Coalition for Responsible Home Education 2017). When looking at families living below the poverty line, the percentages of families that homeschool and families that attend public school are the same. This suggests that homeschooling families tend to have similar income ranges to those in public school. So, homeschool families aren't all living easy lives financially—but they do figure out how to make their budgets work for them (see chapter 7).

Myth: Homeschooling families must have one stay-at-home, non-working parent.

There's definitely no requirement to have one stay-at-home parent. About 47% of homeschooling families have both parents in the labor force (National Center for Education Statistics 2021). Homeschooling families find creative ways to manage their schedules and needs.

Myth: Single parents cannot homeschool.

This is false! In fact, 14 percent of all homeschooling households consist of a single parent in the workforce (Coalition for Responsible Home Education 2017). While situations vary widely, we see that single working parents can and do homeschool.

Managing Schedules

Alicia, homeschool parent and full-time day trader

Alicia, a single mom with full custody of her child, is in her fourth year homeschooling her sixth grade daughter. She shared how she navigates her schedule to make homeschooling work for them. "I mostly work in the evening and at night, which meant when my daughter was in traditional school, I was working when she was home, and so I didn't get to spend very much time with her. When my daughter started third grade, I decided to homeschool her. By changing school up, she spent less time on school, and we could spend time together during the day when I wasn't working. I sleep in the early mornings while she practices figure skating and does her independent schoolwork. After lunch, I help her with all the questions she has on her schoolwork. Then we hang out with friends, have dinner, and when she goes to bed, I start work again. I'm so glad I made this decision to homeschool."

Ways to Make It Work

Families find ways to homeschool despite income level and family structure, even when it might be "unconventional." One of our favorite things about homeschooling is the ability to customize nearly every aspect to make it possible for our unique family. Let's reenvision "schooling" with some customized tweaks for working parents.

Job Flexibility

Who doesn't want job flexibility? Employers may be more open to flexible schedules or remote work since the COVID-19 workplace evolution has expanded the working-from-home field. Finding a work-homeschool balance may require trial and error, but if you allow for some transition time and creative scheduling, you are likely to find stable footing.

Custom Hours

Homeschooling doesn't need to happen between 8 a.m. and 3 p.m. We can homeschool any hours that work for us, whether it's evenings, weekends, or short time periods every day. Sometimes kids are more receptive in the car, in a doctor's office waiting room, or in bed at night (fighting to stay up later!). Mandi's kids have learned to use a lot of fun writing tools in bed at night, writing stories with flashlights and giggles. Adopting a year-round schooling plan is an option that puts less pressure on everyone. Learning should be a lifestyle we enjoy with our children.

Fewer Hours

We do not need to homeschool six and a half hours every day. What can be accomplished in six and a half hours in traditional school can typically be accomplished in one to four hours when homeschooling, depending on our children's developmental age and the number of children being homeschooled. (Please note your state's requirements; some require that you log educational hours.)

Also, no more packing lunches the night before, rushing out the door, sitting in the pick-up line, or walking to the bus stop daily, unless we choose to! There are no teacher conferences, orientation days, back-to-school nights, school-required service hours, or room parent requirements. Instead, we can use that time for our work, developing hobbies, or cuddling our kiddos during a fun movie or read-aloud.

Creative Child Care

Hailey, homeschool parent with three jobs

Single mom Hailey shared how she has three flexible jobs to make homeschooling possible: "I teach a few fitness classes at the YMCA and my girls go to Childwatch (the onsite child care service YMCA provides members and staff). I'm a travel agent and can work anywhere I have Wi-Fi, no restrictions. I started a kid's cooking class business and many of my classes are at different YMCAs where I again utilize Childwatch."

Custom Curriculum

As we've mentioned, there's an abundance of curriculum available to homeschoolers. We choose the curriculum options that work best for our children and for ourselves. We can utilize a checklist, especially for older kids, to ensure they get independent work done on their own, preserving time set aside for working together on other subjects. It's an efficient plan for when we are in meetings. We can also try block or loop scheduling, which are alternative ways to cover all the subjects by using a window of time to cover just one subject. We move on to another subject the next day. See chapter 1 for more content and curriculum ideas.

Support

It can take a village to raise children; tap into yours. Ask for help from your family and friends to find child care when you need to work. My children's favorite day of the week is "Cousin Tuesday" when they spend the entire day with their aunt and four cousins at their home while I teach dance from 9 a.m. to 8 p.m. at the dance studio.

This precious time is spent bonding with their cousins and aunt while they create and perform plays, read books, do schoolwork, play pretend and board games, and make memories together. The most important requirement is that we have confidence in the person who is spending time with our children while we are working.

Outsourcing

It's not all on us. We don't have to be our children's primary learning source. If our kids are with a grandparent or other caregiver while we work, perhaps that person can assist in aspects of learning, while growing a deeper, mutually beneficial bond.

As we discussed in other chapters, online curriculum can be a way for learners to work independently with less oversight by us. Additionally, there are enrichment classes and co-ops that offer drop-off options and can teach one or more subjects or offer collaborative learning experiences. One of our friends takes her children every Wednesday to the San Diego Zoo Safari Park, leaving them there from 9 a.m. to 2 p.m. They get to work with the Safari Park staff, interacting up-close with animals while enjoying the park, focusing on one animal per week, and learning science, some history, Spanish, and art.

Full-Time Work and Full-Time Homeschool

Vanessa, homeschool parent and full-time account manager

Vanessa shared how she navigated multiple children's needs. "My homeschooling journey began in 2015, when I enrolled my oldest son in a local charter school, which provided two days of in-person instruction and three days of home instruction. I had two littles at the time, worked a demanding in-office job, and didn't feel I could manage homeschooling full time. This seemed like a way to experience the best of both worlds. I had the support of my son's teacher, along with the freedom to complete his assignments on a flexible schedule on his home days. I loved being involved in my son's education and gained some confidence through this process.

"By the time my second-born turned five, I was ready to homeschool full time. I had started a position with a new company that agreed to a flexible schedule and didn't require me to work in-office, and I had support from my mother on the days when I did need to venture out for meetings.

"I started out working through a charter school that provided the curriculum and support, but soon realized my daughter was struggling with some of the courses. We now utilize a different charter that provides funds to be applied toward curriculum, extracurricular activities, and technology to support their learning. I feel my children are learning in a way that suits their unique personalities and allows plenty of time to explore their passions and interests. They've made some great friends along the way too!"

The Bottom Line

Ultimately, homeschooling may come down to whether you have the support and job flexibility needed to work and homeschool. For some, this may not be possible even considering all the ways homeschooling can be customized.

But if you do join the many parents who are working and homeschooling, know that you are not alone, and there is a lot of support for homeschoolers. While the juggling act may get tiring at times, and it might feel like a circus, you get to live in the arena, making memories together.

Can-Do Assessment to Explore My Options

- ❏ I can find child care options while I work if needed.
- ❏ I have a flexible job.
- ❏ I can customize our schooling to complement my work hours.
- ❏ I can join homeschooling networks and support systems, whether in-person or online.

Chapter 20

I'm Overwhelmed! How Do I Start Homeschooling?

MANDI

Rocketing into a whole new world of homeschooling can be quite overwhelming. Understanding one's state requirements for homeschooling, learning where to find curriculum, and figuring out how to join a community can be difficult at first. You are not alone! We want to provide a jumping-off point for getting started with homeschooling. (For additional helpful steps and resources, check out the Quick Start Guide in the appendix.)

Find and Follow Your State's Requirements

Reviewing your state's requirements at the Home School Legal Defense Association (HSLDA) website is helpful, especially if withdrawing your child from traditional school requires a formal process. It's important to know your legal rights as a parent. Pairing that information with local homeschooling friends' advice could provide the boost of confidence you need. Your school district may also have an option or program that will help you in this process.

The homeschooling community on social media provides definitions and suggestions for charter schools in your area, independent study programs, umbrella private schools, and other choices available depending on your state.

Ten Tips for New Homeschoolers

1. Homeschooling can be what you want it to be. It doesn't need to mimic traditional school.

2. Make recipes and play games together regularly.

3. Create a "sick bin" for your kids full of special independent activities for when you are ill.

4. Choose an open-and-go curriculum for at least one subject to make your life easier.

5. Share your passion with your kids.

6. Do not compare your homeschool life to others.

7. Start your day by connecting with your kids (gratitude journal, affection, and so on).

8. Ask your kids what they want to learn and make that a priority.

9. New experiences can make a bigger impact than a book; don't rush it.

10. Choose your relationship with your child over forcing a lesson.

Look for social media groups, or check out our website, thecoophomeschool.com/homeschoolhub. Many people in the homeschooling community are eager to answer your questions. You only need to reach out and ask (and fact-check too).

Choose a Curriculum

Curriculum is a helpful tool for getting started. If possible, buy or borrow curriculum long before you implement it so you have time to explore the features and components. It can be quite satisfying to find the teacher scripts, tips, and supply lists to aid in your preparation.

Others' Recommendations

Jessica and I have found some of our curriculum through homeschooling friends' recommendations, teacher recommendations, reviews, and on homeschooling websites (cathyduffyreviews.com, homeschoolcurriculumreview.com, and rainbowresource.com). Many homeschool curriculum reviews can be found in online videos.

Publisher Preferences

If you like a particular reference book or curriculum, find out more about the publisher and explore other materials they offer. I liked a particular grammar curriculum, so I perused that publisher's catalog. Voilà! I found my writing and rhetoric curriculum and my Latin curriculum.

Intimidated by Curriculum

Jessica shared this about her experience getting started: "Curriculum was the most intimidating aspect of homeschooling when I began researching options for my four-year-old daughter. The idea of choosing an all-in-one, open-and-go curriculum was appealing at first as it seemed the least overwhelming. However, once I really looked into learning styles and educational approaches, I realized that an eclectic approach suited my unique daughter best. We needed a simple, straightforward math curriculum, and decided on a spelling curriculum instead of a reading curriculum for language arts. (There are numerous ways to teach reading, and some of us do it through spelling.) We then chose unit studies for science and social studies to allow us to really dive into those topics she was most interested in."

Attend a Homeschool Conference

One significant way I have found some of my favorite curriculum is through conference exhibit halls and sessions. Exhibit halls allow you to review the curriculum, discuss the foundational principles with the publisher or author, and ask questions about customizing the curriculum for your children. The publisher or author helps you understand what you are buying before you buy it. Conferences also put you in the room with other homeschoolers who are eager to discuss their curriculum pros and woes.

Not only can you find curriculum at conferences, you can also go to topical information sessions that interest you. Many conferences have sessions for new homeschoolers as well as sessions that address specific concerns such as college readiness, teaching your child to read, teaching a neurodivergent child, and more. Speakers often have booths in the exhibit hall where you can meet them, ask more questions, and look through their offerings.

Join a Community

We suggest joining a community as an important early step, because it is soul-filling. You don't necessarily need to be part of an official homeschool co-op, but sharing the homeschooling life with friends is something we highly recommend. Plus, creating a customized community for your child and for yourself can be a super fun experience.

There might be a community already formed nearby; if you know anyone in your area who homeschools, reach out to them about joining their group or creating one together. Typically, it's easier to start with families who are already part of a community with you—for example, sports, scouts, your neighborhood, a religious community, an enrichment class, or family friends. You need just one other family to start and give it time to grow. Plan a field trip, read and discuss a book, gather for a holiday celebration, or participate together in an online class. Plan something and begin bonding! (See chapter 9 for how we formed our co-op.)

Just Get Started

Making this leap to homeschool can feel abstract and overwhelming. So ease into it. Try one week in the summer or even just one day during a holiday break. Dip your toes in the water before jumping in.

To get started right away, plan your first week around these ideas:

- Read aloud a classic book (or listen to an audiobook using your library app).
- Play a card or board game and ask your child to keep score.
- Try a new physical activity or skill that only one of you knows well and can teach.
- Go on a hike or take a field trip to a museum.
- Visit the library to check out books that teach content and context related to the chosen book, skill, or museum.
- Plan a playdate or teen hangout with friends.

When I was starting, I messaged a friend who was homeschooling in my state, asking her how to get started. I took her most compelling advice right away: "Attend homeschool conferences." That made a big difference for me in building my enthusiasm and reducing my anxiety. Pick one of these major steps and just begin. Watch for a spark of curious confidence that will come once you start.

Advice from a Working Parent

Nikevia, homeschool parent and lead generation specialist for a publishing company, Maryland

Nikevia, working mother of four homeschooled children, shared with me her challenges and solutions for getting past the overwhelm she felt as a working and homeschool parent. She shared, "Navigating motherhood and a career can have its challenges. I always desired to keep my children home while they were young and have been fortunate to be able to do so as a remote full-time employee. As my oldest was getting closer to age five, I began to feel overwhelmed with how I would work full time and homeschool a kindergartener with four-year-old twins and a two-year-old. Help! My husband and I attended public school so this would be a new journey for us to embark upon.

"I began to look into curriculums and my overwhelmed feeling went through the roof. Who knew there was *so* much out there for homeschool curriculums: classical, Charlotte Mason, Montessori, unit studies, unschooling, and the list goes on. Thank goodness I knew a few families who successfully homeschooled, so I did what I am not always good at doing and asked for help.

"It was extremely helpful to talk with experienced moms who could provide recommendations for how to get started and what type of curriculum would best fit our family with two parents working full time. The best advice I received that I hope will be helpful to others is to find a co-op. What a blessing it was to my children and myself to find a community to connect with that was navigating the world of homeschooling alongside us, that we could learn from and enjoy the experience with.

"The next best advice I received was to start with free and/or used curriculum materials. When you are starting out with homeschooling, you have to give yourself time to see what works best for you and your children. You don't want to make a huge investment in a curriculum that doesn't work for [you], so start slow and use free or inexpensive used materials to test out different methods until you find what works for you.

"The last piece of advice the experienced moms shared with me was to be flexible and just enjoy the journey. With four little ones, working full time, and homeschooling, I truly had to be flexible. I am naturally a type A, overly organized person, so at times this was challenging for me. But some days school just didn't start at 9:00 a.m. sharp. Some days meltdowns from the toddlers only allowed for a 10-minute lesson, a break, and then resuming a little later. I also learned to follow my children's interests. What activities did they really enjoy and what they didn't, and how could I introduce new concepts while learning the types of activities that they liked.

"Starting the homeschool journey can be daunting, but I have found that families who homeschool are excited and eager to help each other. Don't be afraid to ask for help and find a community to enjoy the journey with. You won't regret it!"

Any new thing you begin can be overwhelming and hard at first. You can do hard things, and we are here to help. Head over to our Quick Start Guide, pick one step, and get going. With each step you take, confidence and competence can grow.

You are not alone; there are many experienced homeschoolers to help with any unique situation you may face. Jessica and I wrote this chapter to help you take that very first step, because we know that you can do this.

Can-Do Assessment to Get Started

☐ I can look up state requirements to learn the necessary steps to register my child for homeschooling.

☐ I can complete and submit the documents the state requires.

☐ I can pick one way to learn about curriculum.

☐ I can look into attending a homeschool conference near me.

☐ There is one homeschooling family or friend that I can ask about forming a community together or about joining their community.

☐ I can make a list of three things I can do to get started.

Conclusion
Confident and Free

JESSICA AND MANDI

Having hesitations about homeschooling is understandable! We wrote this book to help you find your confidence while connecting with your children in a multitude of ways. Homeschooling has been a life-changing choice for us that continues to build the deep family connection we wanted, and we know you can have that too. We've addressed many hesitations you may have about homeschooling by offering research-based answers, personal stories from homeschoolers around the United States, and creative ideas. However, the most beautiful part of homeschooling for us is the freedom we have to customize our entire life to fit our family's desires. Homeschooling looks different for every family, and sometimes even for each child within a family. But for us, homeschooling isn't only about an educational decision; it's bigger than that— it's about living a lifestyle of choice. And we both believe this is the best choice for our families.

While there are many options for curriculum, enrichment, and community activities, you have no obligation to use them. *You* get to choose the intensity of study. *You* get to choose if and how busy you are running your children around to activities. *You* get to choose to spend a season just staying home, snuggling, reading, and developing a craft. *You* get to choose to spend a month on the road, camping, sightseeing, and learning on location. Not every day will be what you wanted or expected, not even every week or month. That's okay. We all have good days and bad days no matter what we try. But like many other worthwhile experiences in life, big or small, trials beget triumph. Experiencing failure is part of the growing process. And if we are asking our children to grow, we need to grow with them, even when it's inconvenient or uncomfortable. As many of us know, a great deal of growth can happen when we step outside our comfort zones.

We all struggle with the challenges of parenting our children, and homeschooling isn't any different. In some scenarios, it *is* the harder lifestyle. But if you are asking, "What is best for my child?" or "What is best for me?", we say that's not the ultimate question you need to ask. The question you need to ask yourself and your family unit is: "What is best for our *family*?" What lifestyle does your family need to live their best life? We cannot answer that question for you. The good news is that whatever you do choose, it isn't permanent. You can try a lifestyle change to see how it fits. And even if you find the perfect fit, there will be plenty more opportunities for questioning and hesitating throughout your parenting journey.

Our Joys in a Snapshot

Mandi

My family is living our best life because we homeschool. On our home days, I get to wake up and listen to my favorite '80s music while my kids cuddle our kitty, play with LEGO bricks, or code game apps. Usually, my youngest hops in bed with me and we snuggle as she shares last night's bedtime reading or writing, her dreams, and lingering thoughts from the day before. This time at home is precious to me.

We enjoy a peaceful morning together with gratitude. We spend our day learning new games and curriculum, laughing, arguing, striving, and growing, and sometimes that all happens in our pajamas. After my spouse gets home from work, our youngest nestles next to him while he picks up the current family read-aloud. As he settles in for the highlight of his day, I relax or work on my side hustle. Sometimes we have a family dinner, and sometimes we don't. But we live our life together the way we want it, with complete freedom and unconditional love. And that is all we need.

Jessica

Homeschooling has allowed me to do all the things I'm passionate about. I am able to spend an incredible amount of time with my children, and since 2020, my husband has been working from home and is a huge part of our everyday experiences. We are able to customize our children's education, take a three-week road trip during the off-season, and focus on developing our children's interests. As a dance educator for twenty years, I am able to balance working with homeschooling, and my kids get to see me pursue my career and hobby alongside motherhood. I have been present to celebrate every educational milestone and all their joys and heartaches, big or small.

One Final Note

Our snapshots won't look the same as yours. They should look different because the homeschooling lifestyle can be what you picture. You get to set the stage, pick the people and the props—and then create a picture of whatever you want. With your questions addressed, it is our sincere hope that if you are thinking of homeschooling, you choose to do it and do so confidently. Whether you are a new parent, a working parent, feeling unqualified, or worried about your child's eccentricities, you can do this. You can homeschool if you truly want to.

Quick Start Guide

You might be feeling various emotions at this point, so let us help build your confidence with six definitive steps for starting this new parenting endeavor. With each step, we provide ideas that you can choose from to customize for your family. This Quick Start Guide takes the guesswork out of getting started; enjoy your new adventure!

Step 1—Know the Legal Requirements

Every state has its own laws and resources for homeschooling that range from no regulation to high regulation. Many states require some of the following: pull your child from the school district, complete a form, sign up with an independent study program, or become a one-family private school. Some states require nothing at all. It depends on your state.

- Research at websites such as the very helpful Home School Legal Defense Association (HSLDA) or your state's department of education to find out what kind of registration your state requires for homeschooling.

- Ask a local homeschooling friend about the required process and opportunities available in your area.

- Use your browser to search your state's name and "homeschooling," and you will likely see the top sites with information about the process, time line, potential umbrella schools/private schools, and public charter schools available for homeschooling in your area.

Step 2—Change Your Perspective

Welcome to the whole new world of homeschooling. Take a few weeks to spend time *deschooling*. Here are some considerations to change how you think about educating your child:

- Write a short mission statement to get started. Why are you homeschooling, and what do you and your child want from it? Dream fun and dream big. Use your mission to measure your choices in this world of freedom and endless options.

- View the entire day as a learning opportunity. Your child's brain is always working and growing, and not just from 8 a.m. to 3 p.m. Not all activities are equal in quality, but knowing the research we've shared about free time and play should take the pressure off of you.

- Tune into your child's moods and needs throughout the day and start gauging their most receptive time of day for learning. You do not need to replicate the traditional school experience at home. You can pick the best times of day for learning activities and bookwork.

- Prioritize fun! Unique learning opportunities, special time together, outings with friends, new experiences . . . do them all. Set the tone early that this will be enriching, heart-fulfilling, and mind-boggling, with some good solid work too.

- As a fun challenge, you can start deschooling by writing down every traditional school restraint and then try to do the opposite for this period of time. No raising hands to go to the bathroom or get water. Sit where you want—sofas, floors, and beds only! Sleep in. Stay up late. Do not write names at the top of any paper. No grading. Just be together with open and curious hearts. Deschooling can help free you to engage your child in the way that fits the life you both want.

To get started during the first week, try any or all of the following:

- Ask your children to each pick books they want to read and commit to reading one of those too.

- Build something together (toy bricks, forts, decks of cards).

- Read every picture book on a bookshelf (at home or at a library).
- Design a mall scavenger hunt and invite friends to join in, with ice cream as the final stop.
- Carve statues from bars of soap.
- Play charades.
- Take a nature walk.
- Offer to help a neighbor.
- Take local transportation to a museum with friends.
- Spend time with extended family.
- Try a new recipe for dinner and teach new kitchen skills.
- Make a how-to video.

Step 3—Find Your Content

This can be a long but fun process. Take your time and enjoy learning about your child's interests together. To get started right away, pick a couple of the following activities:

- Ask your child what they are interested in learning and explore that.
- List and plan visits to inexpensive or free educational places your child wants to see (local museums, parks and trails, playgrounds, historical sites, and so on).
- Go to the library and spend unlimited time looking at books. Check out the books your child is excited about. Look at them together or start a conversation about them. Does your child want to go back and get more?
- Start a read-aloud with your child that is appropriate for their development and interests.
- Make a list of documentaries that would be appropriate for your child's development and watch them together.

Thankfully, it's a big homeschooling world. So tackle a few of these options once you feel you have your feet under you:

- Make a budget. If it's time to start buying curriculum or planning enriching activities and group field trips, know what your limits are and prioritize accordingly.

- Consider trying an educational subscription box. Look up popular ones and use your child's interests and development as your guide. Some favorites of ours are Kiwi Co's Kiwi Crate, Bitsbox, Universal Yums, Raddish Kids, and Crunch Labs. Do not sign up for an entire year; just try it for one to three months to see if it's a good fit.

- Order a children's magazine like *National Geographic for Kids* or *The Week Junior* for the shortest duration allowed (to review it). Pick one that will be fun to discuss and possibly spur further research and activities.

- Explore your state's academic standards if you wish to see a generally accepted list of suggested content and skills for grade levels below, at, and above your child's.

- Join Facebook homeschool groups and ask questions to see trends in favorite curriculum among seasoned homeschoolers.

- Research credible websites that review curriculum, such as Homeschool Curriculum Review (homeschoolcurriculumreview.com).

- Ask homeschooling friends if you can peruse their curriculum.

- Start researching various homeschooling approaches, such as Charlotte Mason, classical education, unschooling, eclectic, and others. Different types of curriculum include unit studies, box curriculum, and more. Some are "open-and-go," requiring no preparation. Take your time to figure out what might work for you at this early stage.

Step 4—Research Enrichment

Search for homeschool enrichment programs that pique your child's interest, such as music lessons, farm schools, theater, literature-based courses, sports classes, STEM labs, robotics clubs, and more.

- Pick one enrichment within your budget that your child will be excited about attending, and sign up.

- For online options, take a look at Outschool.com and try a class. You can sit with your child and learn whether it piques their interest.

Step 5—Find a Supportive Community

Don't do this alone! Try one or two of these options:

- Be open to meeting new people and forming new relationships.
- Join social media homeschooling groups in your area. They offer meet-ups and field trips that you can attend to connect with other homeschoolers. Invite people to meet you at a local park.
- Search online and register for an upcoming homeschool conference in your area. Attend with enthusiasm and friendliness. There are plenty of potential new friends there if you take the initiative.
- Reach out to people on location at your child's activities. There might be more homeschoolers than you realize.

Step 6—Think of You

Carve out some time in the upcoming weeks to do the following:

- Schedule personal time: self-care, meditation, spiritual time, personal or professional development.
- Read or listen to a book about homeschooling or parenting that you feel will equip you in one new way and grow your confidence or excitement for homeschooling.
- Attend an upcoming homeschool conference and spend time in the exhibit hall to learn what publishers and companies have to offer in this new world. Find what is exciting to you.
- Give yourself grace. Trying something new can be invigorating but also hard. You won't get it perfect right away. We all make mistakes.

Read to Inspire and Grow Confidence

Brave Learner: Finding Everyday Magic in Homeschool, Learning, and Life, by Julie Bogart (TarcherPerigee 2019)—A fun book that helps the reader think outside the education box by offering a mindset shift, creative and practical ideas, and a few fundamental educational concepts for a magical homeschool life.

Free to Learn: Why Unleashing the Instinct to Play Will Make Our Children Happier, More Self-Reliant, and Better Students for Life, by Peter Gray (Basic Books 2013)—An empowering book that demonstrates that the primary way children learn is through free play.

How Children Learn, 50th anniversary edition, by John Holt (Da Capo Lifelong Books 2017)—An insightful exploration of the natural ways children learn and how adults can encourage those abilities.

The Read-Aloud Family: Making Meaningful and Lasting Connections with Your Kids, by Sarah MacKenzie (Zondervan 2018)—With vetted book lists filtered for age ranges and interests, parenting tips, and ideas for nurturing compassion, this resource provides how-tos for connecting with your children through books.

The Self-Driven Child: The Science and Sense of Giving Your Kids More Control Over Their Lives, by William Stixrud and Ned Johnson (Penguin Life 2019)—A fascinating telling of real stories and synthesis of research that will teach parents how to help their children make their own decisions and be internally motivated to be their authentic selves.

Enjoy! Designing a customized plan of action that interests you and your children is the key to making this new journey all yours.

Glossary

academics—subjects that require studying and reasoning useful for philosophical ideas, debate, and knowledge; typically includes math, language arts, history, and science. Academics can be taught through textbooks, workbooks, and other methods that people often associate with school, but they can also be taught through cooking, travel, life experiences, and more.

accommodations—changes to how the content is delivered to fit the needs of a neurodivergent or gifted learner. For example, offering a longer time period for the same tests and assignments, or assigning an audiobook instead of the reading book assigned to other students. (Also see *modifications,* which refers to the actual content that is delivered.)

block scheduling—allocating a long period or block of time for one subject (e.g., two to three hours).

boxed curriculum (all-in-one)—a comprehensive program providing grade-leveled scope and sequence, textbooks, assessments, projects, and time lines with very specific, day-by-day instructions to both parent and student.

Charlotte Mason (homeschool method)—based on the teaching of Charlotte Mason, a nineteenth-century homeschooling pioneer, this method focuses on short study periods, nature studies, memorization, and reading—especially "living books."

charter school—a publicly funded school that operates as a school of choice independently of the state school system. Charter schools can meet five days per week like traditional schools, they can use a hybrid in-class and at-home schedule, or they can be full-time homeschool or independent study charters.

classical education—one of the most popular homeschool styles, this method often employs "Great Books" and the "Trivium" in a chronological reading plan to study subject areas historically. Often included are Greek and Latin learning.

co-op—a group of homeschool families that has organized meetings. Some are formal co-ops where the parents alternate teaching lessons to the group. Others are less formal and meet for playdates, field trips, and other educational opportunities.

curriculum—what we teach our children, which includes planned educational lessons and activities; a collection of information found in books, media, and magazines combined with experiences and activities on a subject that aid in teaching important skills and knowledge over a length of time.

deschooling—the period of time a child (and parent) needs to adjust and recalibrate their mindset when going from traditional schooling to homeschooling, which may entail learning to allow natural curiosities to grow organically while taking an extended break from more teacher-led, formal lessons.

eclectic—often called "relaxed homeschooling," eclectic homeschoolers may pull from many methods, as the main objective is to educate their own individual child rather than ascribe to a single method.

education—the *process* of taking in and storing information in our brains to enlighten and form our foundational perspectives, values, ethics, skills, and relationships. Education can be delivered formally through direct instruction or guidance—with books, games, experiences, field trips, technology, and teamwork—or informally through experiencing life's daily challenges, travel, reading, and relationships.

enrichment—classes, programs, and activities provided by the parent, family, or other educators to offer electives, extracurriculars, or in-depth study of a particular topic or subject.

homeschool method—the approach for education at home. Includes Charlotte Mason, classical, Montessori, unschooling, and more.

learning—the knowledge or skill *acquired* through a lesson or informative process.

learning disability—a disorder that affects the brain's ability to learn in a typical way.

loop scheduling—rotating through content according to a list of subjects rather than on a daily schedule.

mastery-based learning—when a student must gain full understanding (mastery) of a skill, lesson, or activity before moving on to learn the next one.

micro-school—a customized classroom environment mimicking the traditional school for which families hire a qualified educator to teach specific subjects to a small group of children.

modifications—changes to the content being delivered to meet the needs of neurodivergent and gifted learners. Examples include offering a different or shortened test or homework requirement, or assigning a different (or abridged) book. (Also see *accommodations,* which refers to how the content is delivered.)

Montessori—a humanistic, student-based approach to learning developed by Maria Montessori in the twentieth century. This method utilizes large, unstructured time blocks, free movement, multi-grade teaching, and individualized learning plans.

neurodivergent—an umbrella term for people with neurological struggles and strengths, such as dyslexia, ADHD, ASD, and more.

open-and-go curriculum—curriculum that provides almost everything you need in one, and you do not need to prepare ahead of time to present the material.

Orton-Gillingham approach—a multisensory approach to teaching reading to children who have reading difficulties such as dyslexia.

private school affidavit (PSA)—a form completed online and submitted to the state and/or school district to create a private school. In some states, a PSA is required to claim your home as a private school in which you will provide home instruction separate from the public offering.

private school umbrella—an entity (often a private school) that oversees homeschooling families and may provide administrative and educational support.

roadschooling—homeschooling while the family travels, be it a road trip, RV living, or other travel, to focus on the learning experiences that the world has to offer.

school-at-home—using the traditional school approach at home; this model is often centered around complete curriculum packages based on grades and academic school years.

state standards—established lists of academic requirements arranged by subject area and grade level, set by each state's board of education.

supplemental resources—nonrequired instructional materials.

teaching—the *sharing* of knowledge, skills, or experiences through teacher-centered (what the teacher decides to teach) or student-centered (what the student chooses to learn) means.

traditional schools—public, private, or parochial schools and classrooms that educate in defined spaces for an average of five days per week and 180 days per year, using authority figures (teachers) and groups of children assigned to grade levels who learn together with their peers with minimal parental influence on site.

unit study—topically based educational studies that use a theme to teach multiple subjects.

unschooling—a student-centered, freeform learning model based largely on the work of John Holt. Unschooling is unconventional and individualistic and encourages a learn-as-you-go education.

References

Accredited Schools Online. 2023. "College Application Guide for Home Schooled Students." Last modified October 17, 2023. accreditedschoolsonline.org/resources/homeschooler-college-applications/.

American Psychological Association. 2019. "Top 20 Principles for Early Childhood Teaching and Learning." Coalition for Psychology in Schools and Education. apa.org/ed/schools/teaching-learning/top-twenty/early-childhood.

Arga, Hana Sakura Putu, Faridillah Fahmi Nurfurqon, and Riga Zahara Nurani. 2020. "Improvement of Creative Thinking Ability of Elementary Teacher Education Students in Utilizing Traditional Games in Social Studies Learning." *Elementary School Forum (Mimbar Sekolah Dasar)* 7 (2): 235–250. eric.ed.gov/?id=EJ1280241.

Barkan, Steven E. 2011. *Sociology: Understanding and Changing the Social World, Comprehensive Edition.* Boston: FlatWorld.

Benson, Kyle. n.d. "The Magic Relationship Ratio, According to Science." *The Gottman Institute.* Accessed April 17, 2024. gottman.com/blog/the-magic-relationship-ratio-according-science/.

BestColleges. 2023. "The 7 Best Extracurricular Activities for College Applications." Last modified May 5, 2023. bestcolleges.com/blog/best-extracurriculars-college-applications/.

Bielick, Stacey, Kathryn Chandler, and Stephen P. Broughman. 2001. "Homeschooling in the United States: 1999." National Household Education Surveys Program: Statistical Analysis Report, July 2001. US Department of Education. Washington, DC: National Center for Education Statistics. nces.ed.gov/pub 001/2001033.pdf.

Bracamonte, Micaela. 2010. "Twice Exceptional Students: Who They Are and What They Need." Davidson Institute, *2e Newsletter.* March 18, 2010. davidsongifted.org/gifted-blog/2e-students-who-they-are-and-what-they-need/.

California Department of Education. n.d. "San Diego County Charter Schools." Charter Schools in California Counties. Accessed April 17, 2024. cde.ca.gov/ds/si/cs/ap1/countyresults.aspx?id=37.

Campbell, Janice. 2018. *Transcripts Made Easy: The Homeschooler's Guide to High School Paperwork.* Ashland, VA: Everyday Education.

Claybourn, Cole. 2023. "CLEP Exams: What to Know." *US News & World Report,* March 14, 2023. usnews.com/education/best-colleges/articles/clep-exams-what-to-know.

Cleveland Clinic. 2022. "Neurodivergent." Last reviewed June 2, 2022. my.clevelandclinic.org/health/symptoms/23154-neurodivergent.

Coalition for Responsible Home Education. n.d. "Homeschooling & Disabilities." Accessed April 17, 2024. responsiblehomeschooling.org/guides/resources-for-homeschool-parents/disabilities/.

———. 2017. "Homeschool Demographics." National Center for Education Statistics. Last modified November 2017. responsiblehomeschooling.org/research/summaries/homeschool-demographics.

———. 2021. "The Homeschool Community Has a Problem with Disabilities (and How to Fix it)." Last modified November 2, 2023. responsiblehomeschooling.org/the-homeschool-community-has-a-problem-with-disabilities-and-how-to-fix-it/.

Cogan, Michael F. 2010. "Exploring Academic Outcomes of Homeschooled Students." *Journal of College Admission* Summer 2010: 19–25. files.eric.ed.gov/fulltext/EJ893891.pdf.

College Board. n.d. "Can I Take the AP Exam if I Haven't Taken an AP Course?" AP Students. Accessed April 17, 2024. apstudents.collegeboard.org/faqs/can-i-take-ap-exam-if-i-havent-taken-ap-course.

CollegeData. n.d. "What Do Colleges Look for In Students?" Accessed April 17, 2024. collegedata.com/resources/getting-in/what-do-colleges-look-for-in-students.

Council of Chief State School Officers. n.d. "Tools and Resources for Standards Implementation." Accessed April 17, 2024. ccsso.org/tools-and-resources-standards-implementation.

Davidson Institute. 2021a. "Twice Exceptional: Definition, Characteristics & Identification." May 31, 2021. davidsongifted.org/gifted-blog/twice-exceptional-definition-characteristics-identification/.

———. 2021b. "What Is Giftedness? Gifted Testing and Identification." July 12, 2021. davidsongifted.org/gifted-blog/what-is-giftedness/.

Duvall, Steven. 2022. "Homeschooling Demographics Continue to Change Rapidly." HSLDA (Home School Legal Defense Association), June 14, 2022. hslda.org/post/homeschooling-demographics-continue-to-change-rapidly.

Ericsson, Anders K., and Robert Pool. 2016. *Peak: Secrets from the New Science of Expertise.* New York: Houghton Mifflin Harcourt.

Fitzgerald, Meghan. n.d. "Why Kids' Vestibular Systems Need Exercise Every Day." Tinkergarten. Accessed April 17, 2024. tinkergarten.com/blog/a-hidden-sense-what-is-the-vestibular-sense.

Fobbs, Leslie. 2018. "Homeschooling Heroes: The Hanson Brothers." Homeschooling Heroes, May 15, 2018. homeschoolingheroes.com/how-to-teach-at-home/homeschooling-heroes-the-hanson-brothers.

Gatto, John Taylor. (1992) 2017. *Dumbing Us Down: The Hidden Curriculum of Compulsory Schooling*, 25th Anniversary Edition. Gabriola Island, BC: New Society Publishers.

Generous Family. 2023. "Family Generosity Series Parent Guide (Teens)." *Generous Family*, 2023. generousfamily.com/family-resources/#downloadables.

Goleman, Daniel. 1988. "Erikson, in His Own Old Age, Expands His View of Life." *The New York Times*, June 14, 1988. archive.nytimes.com/www.nytimes.com/books/99/08/22/specials/erikson-old.html.

Gonzalez, Brittany. 2023. "30 Benefits of a Neurodiversity-Affirming Home Education (NDAHE)." NeuroGrooves. April 15, 2023. linkedin.com/pulse/30-benefits-neurodiversity-affirming-homeschooling-gonzalez-m-ed-/.

Gray, Peter. 2013. *Free to Learn: Why Unleashing the Instinct to Play Will Make Our Children Happier, More Self-Reliant, and Better Students for Life*. New York: Basic Books.

———. 2016. "Alison Gopnik's Advice to Parents: Stop Parenting!" *Psychology Today*, August 19, 2016. psychologytoday.com/us/blog/freedom-learn/201608/alison-gopnik-s-advice-parents-stop-parenting.

Gray, Peter, Autumn Erdahl Solomon, and Leah Tatgenhorst. 2022. "Public Libraries as Centers for Play: A Survey and Case Examples" *American Journal of Play* 14 (2): 131–148. files.eric.ed.gov/fulltext/EJ1359210.pdf.

GreatSchools. 2023. "Why Are Standards Important?" Last modified January 23, 2023. greatschools.org/gk/articles/why-are-standards-important/.

Holt, John. (1967) 2017. *How Children Learn*, 50th Anniversary Edition. New York: Da Capo Press.

Howard, Shellee. 2017. *How to Send Your Student to College Without Losing Your Mind or Your Money*. Self-published.

Hughey, Judy. 2020. "Individual Personalized Learning." *Educational Considerations* 46 (2):10. doi.org/10.4148/0146-9282.2237.

Kessler, Colleen. 2021. "Homeschooling My Gifted Child: Here's Why It Was the Best Choice," *Simple Homeschool*. April 20, 2021. simplehomeschool.net/homeschooling-my-gifted-child/.

Klicka, Christopher J. 2007. "Homeschooled Students Excel in College (Special Report)." Home School Legal Defense Association, August 23, 2007. silo.tips/download/homeschooled-students-excel-in-college.

Kolb, David A. 2015. *Experiential Learning: Experience as the Source of Learning and Development*. 2nd ed. Upper Saddle River, NJ: Pearson Education.

Kwateng-Clark, Danielle. 2020. "Serena Williams Said She Never Felt Broke Living in Compton." *Essence*, October 26, 2020. essence.com/celebrity/serena-williams-uninterrupted/.

Lake, Rebecca. 2022. "The Cost of Homeschooling: How Families Can Afford This Popular Educational Option." *Investopedia,* May 16, 2022. investopedia.com/the-cost-of-homeschooling-5199813.

Lansford, Jennifer E. 2020. "Parents' Involvement in Children's Education: Back to School (Online)." *Psychology Today,* August 15, 2020. psychologytoday.com/us/blog/parenting-and-culture/202008/parents-involvement-in-children-s-education.

Lee, Laura J. 2016. "Cutting Class: Experiences of Gifted Adolescents Who Switched to Homeschooling." *Home School Researcher* 32 (3). nheri.org/home-school-researcher-cutting-class-experiences-of-gifted-adolescents-who-switched-to-homeschooling/.

McQuiggan, Meghan, and Mahi Megra. 2017. "Parent and Family Involvement in Education: Results from the National Household Education Surveys Program of 2016 (NCES 2017-102)." US Department of Education. Washington, DC: National Center for Education Statistics. nces.ed.gov/pubsearch/pubsinfo.asp?pubid=2017102.

Montes, Guillermo. 2015. "The Social and Emotional Health of Homeschooled Students in the United States: A Population-Based Comparison with Publicly Schooled Students Based on the National Survey of Children's Health, 2007." *Home School Researcher* 31 (1). nheri.org/home-school-researcher-the-social-and-emotional-health-of-homeschooled-students-in-the-united-states-a-population-based-comparison-with-publicly-schooled-students-based-on-the-national-survey-of-child/.

Morin, Amanda, and Emily Kircher-Morris. 2023. "Is Your School Welcoming to Neurodiverse Students?" *The Learning Professional,* 44 (5): 46-48.

The Nectar Group. 2023. "Teaching with the Brain in Mind: Lessons from Neuroscience." Webinar, May 23, 2023.

Newman, Paul. 2013. "Serena Williams: I Was the Runt, But Tough Upbringing Made Me the World-Beater I Am Now." *Independent US Edition,* June 10, 2013. independent.co.uk/sport/tennis/serena-williams-i-was-the-runt-but-tough-upbringing-made-me-the-worldbeater-i-am-now-8651400.html.

National Center for Education Statistics. 2020. "Table 1.1. Minimum Number of Instructional Days and Hours in the School Year, Minimum Number of Hours Per School Day, and School Start/Finish Dates, By State: 2020." State Education Practices. nces.ed.gov/programs/statereform/tab1_1-2020.asp.

National Home Education Research Institute. 2023. "Research Facts on Homeschooling." March 11, 2023. nheri.org/research-facts-on-homeschooling/.

National Home Education Surveys Program. n.d. "Percentage of Students Ages 5 Through 17 in Grades Kindergarten Through 12 or the Equivalent Who Were Enrolled in School or Homeschooled, by Disability Status: 2011–12." National Center for Education Statistics. Accessed April 17, 2024. nces.ed.gov/nhes/tables/enrolled_homeschool.asp.

Paolini, Christopher. 2015. "My Experience with Homeschooling." paolini.net. Last modified May 29, 2015. paolini.net/2015/05/29/my-experience-with-homeschooling/.

Pruett, Kyle D. 2019. "Playful Learning Beyond the Classroom: Non-School Structured Setting Stimulate Learning, Strengthen Executive Function." *Psychology Today*, November 22, 2019. psychologytoday.com/us/blog/once-upon-child/201911/playful-learning-beyond-the-classroom.

Ray, Brian D. 2004. "Homeschoolers on to College: What Research Shows Us." *Journal of College Admission* Fall 2004: 5–11. files.eric.ed.gov/fulltext/EJ682480.pdf.

———. 2011. "A Brief Review of Homeschooled Students in College by Bolle-Brummond and Wessel."*HomeSchoolResearcher*26(3).nheri.org/home-school-researcher-a-brief-review-of-homeschooled-students-in-college-by-bolle-brummond-and-wessel/.

Rosenshine, Barak V. 2015. "How Time Is Spent in Elementary Classrooms." *Journal of Classroom Interaction* 50.1: 41–53. files.eric.ed.gov/fulltext/EJ1100409.pdf.

Stixrud, William, and Ned Johnson. 2019. *The Self-Driven Child: The Science and Sense of Giving Your Kids More Control Over Their Lives*. New York: Penguin Books.

Treleaven, Lisa M. 2022. "Quantitative Insights into the Academic Outcomes of Homeschools from the Classic Learning Test." *Home School Researcher* 38 (1). nheri.org/wp-content/uploads/2022/12/HSR381-Treleaven-article-only.pdf.

University of California. n.d. "After You Apply." Accessed April 17, 2024. admission.universityofcalifornia.edu/how-to-apply/applying-as-a-freshman/after-you-apply.

US Bureau of Labor Statistics. 2023. "Employment Characteristics of Families—2022." News Release, April 19, 2023. bls.gov/news.release/pdf/famee.pdf.

US Department of Education. 2019. "Homeschooling in the United States: Results from the 2012 and 2016 Parent and Family Involvement Survey (PFINHES: 2012 and 2016)." National Household Education Surveys Program, December 2019. National Center for Education Statistics. nces.ed.gov/pub X020/2020001.pdf.

Wedge, Marilyn. 2014. "Is Free Play Essential for Learning?" *Psychology Today*, July 2, 2014. psychologytoday.com/us/blog/suffer-the-children/201407/is-free-play-essential-learning.

West, Cindy. 2023. "101 Reasons to Homeschool Gifted Children." *Our Journey Westward*, February 9, 2023. ourjourneywestward.com/reasons-to-homeschool-gifted-children/.

Widiger, T. A., and W. L. Gore. 2016. "Personality Disorders." *Encyclopedia of Mental Health, Second Edition*. Academic Press, 270–77. doi.org/10.1016/B978-0-12-397045-9.00092-6.

Wooden, John, and Steve Jamison. 1997. *Wooden: A Lifetime of Observations and Reflections On and Off the Court*. New York: McGraw Hill.

Index

A

academics
  about, 58
  access to resources for, 111–113
  classroom/group learning and, 113–114
  in a homeschooling day, 57, 59–60
  test scores and, 109
ACT exam, 155, 156
ADHD (attention deficit/hyperactivity disorder), 163, 172
Advanced Placement classes, 112, 153
adventures, 13–14, 32, 77–78
all-in-one (boxed) curriculum, 10, 148
amusement parks, 66, 78
antisocial behavior, 137
anxious learners, 31–32
AP classes and exams, 112, 153, 155–156
arts, the, 59, 87–88
assessments, 170–171
audiobooks, 15, 45, 76, 189
autism spectrum disorder, 163, 169
autonomy, 30, 61, 172

B

band, school, 87–88
block scheduling, 71
boxed curriculum, 10, 148
Boys and Girls Club, 54, 78, 89
budget, homeschooling on a, 75–80

C

careers, of parents, 117, 119–120
celebrations, 82–85
Charlotte Mason (homeschool method), 26, 190, 198
charter schools, 79, 85, 112–113
child(ren). *See also* learners; learning
  activities and interests pursued by, 62–63, 65–66
  autonomy in, 61
  concerns about "falling behind," 145–151
  daily scheduling and

  personalities of, 68–69
  designing their own curriculum, 27
  fitting in the homeschool community, 96
  gifted, 161, 163–165, 167–168, 170–173
  homeschooling an only, 143–144
  learning about interests of, 197
  socialization of, 136–144
  statistics on number of homeschooled, 95
  twice-exceptional, 163–164
classical education (homeschool style), 26, 190, 198
CLEP (College Level Examination Program) exam, 155, 156
clubs, 89, 114
coach, parent in the role of, 38
college degrees, 23, 152–160
Common Core standards, 146
Community. *See also* homeschool community
  benefits of, 93
  for teens and tweens, 97
community college courses, 113, 155
competitions, academic, 114
conferences, 123–124, 173, 188, 199
cooking together, 104
co-ops
  benefit of joining, 190
  celebrations with, 83
  field trips with, 14
  group learning through, 114
  making friends through, 123
  socializing with friends through, 67
  working families using, 183
cultural celebrations and festivals, 83, 105
curriculum
  about, 9
  advantages of, 11
  as an educational tool, 171
  budget-friendly, 77

  children designing their own, 27
  choosing a, 186–187
  knowing the, 8–9
  packaging of, 10–11
  types of, 10
curriculum schedules, falling behind the, 148–149

D

daily routine schedule, 69–70
decision-making, involving children in, 39, 52
defiant learners, 34
deschooling, 35, 50, 196
developmental delays, 147, 166
diploma, high school, 157
disabilities, children with, 162–163, 168–170
diversity, 90, 98, 101–108
dual enrollment, 155
dyslexia, 162, 172

E

educational gaps, 151
education, definition of, 58
enrichment, 12–17
  field trips/adventures, 13–14
  group learning experiences, 114
  in-person opportunities, 111
  low-cost, 77–78
  online, 112
  researching programs for, 198–199
enrichment centers and schools, 66
ethnicity, homeschool community and, 101–102
experiential learning, 52–54
extracurricular activities, 116, 153–154, 158. *See also* enrichment

F

faith-based celebrations and holidays, 83
faith-based curriculum, 9, 10, 18
family members
  helping teach a sibling to read, 31

mentored learning with, 66
sharing homeschooling load
    with, 18–20, 47, 48
working families getting
    support from, 182–183
family time, homeschooling providing
    opportunities for, 128
field trips, 13–14, 120, 189.
    See also adventures
freedom, when choosing to
    homeschool, 127–128
free play, 120, 140
free resources, 75–77
free time, 27, 61–64
friends(hips). *See also*
    homeschool community
    of parents, 122–124
    providing time for children to
        spend with, 67
    teen huddle and, 97

G

games, 18, 64, 171, 186
gifted learners, 161, 163–165,
    167–168, 170–173
GPAs, 160
grade-level curriculum, 10, 11
graduation rate, 160

H

hands-on-kits and experiences, 16,
    167
History, learning, 59, 60
homeschool community. *See also*
    co-ops
    benefits of having a, 93–94, 98
    clubs and groups through, 89
    diversity in, 98, 101–102, 106
    finding a, 199
    receiving help from, 185–186
    serving others, 98–99
homeschool day, structure of, 57–74
    for academics, 59–60
    free time, 61–64
    friendship time, 67
    intentional time together, 64–65
    "me time" for parents in, 120–122
    mission statement for, 66–67
    schedules, examples of, 69–71
    for working families, 180,
        181–182

homeschooling
    benefits of, 166–168, 192–194
    getting started with, 185–191,
        196–197
    as a lifestyle choice, 192
Home School Legal Defense
    Association (HSLDA), 113,
    147, 158, 185, 195
honors classes, 112, 153

I

inadequate, learners who feel, 33–34
independent learners, 30
independent study programs, 112, 153
Individuals with Disabilities
    Education Act, 168, 170
in-person enrichment, 111
in-person instruction, 40
International Baccalaureate (IB)
    classes, 112, 153
internships, 115
introversion, 137

K

Khan Academy, 76, 112

L

languages, learning, 59, 104–105
leadership opportunities, 88–89
learners
    anxious and perfectionist, 31–32
    strong-willed and independent,
        30
    who are defiant and difficult, 34
    who are not interested, 32
    who do not want a parent to
        teach them, 35
    who do not want to be
        homeschooled, 35–36
    who feel inadequate, 33–34
    who think and learn
        independently, 33
learning
    celebrations for, 84–85
    definition, 58
    experiential, 52–54
    group, 113–114
    importance of relationships for, 24
    mentored, 66
    personalized, 129–130, 132
    on their own, 26–27

    through adventures, 13–14
    tools for helping, 37–41
learning disabilities (LD), 163
learning spaces, 50–56
legal requirements and rights, 185,
    195
lesson plans, writing, 148–149
letters of recommendation, 158
libraries, 51, 76, 89, 111

M

mastery-based curriculum, 10, 11
math, 33, 59, 60
mental health, 47, 48
mentored learning, 66
mindset, changing your, 8, 35, 38
mission statement, 67–68, 150–151,
    196
movement, during a homeschool
    day, 64
multisensory learning, 171, 172
museums, 50, 65, 77–78, 107, 189
music/music lessons, 59, 65, 87–88

N

National Home Education
    Research Institute (NHERI),
    75, 157
naysayers, 174–177
neurodivergent children, 161, 163,
    164–167, 171

O

online curriculum, 11, 40, 183
online enrichment, 112
only children, 143–144
open-and-go curriculum, 10
Orton-Gillingham approach, 171, 172
Outschool, 66, 112
outsourced learning, 65–66

P

parent(s)
    ability to teach their children,
        22–23, 25–26
    on benefits of homeschooling,
        126–127, 131–132, m139–140
    careers of, 117, 119–120
    changing their perspective, 196
    children not wanting to be
        taught by their, 35

developing their teaching skills, 26

friendships of, 122–124

getting started with homeschooling, 185–191, 196–197

homeschooling without a co-parent, 176

learning with their children, 8–9, 28

mental health of, 47

"me time" for, 120–122

personal values and experiences of, 17–18

role modeling by, 38

self-care by, 46–47

single, 178, 180

stay-at-home, 180

working, 178–184

parenting, teaching and, 22–23

"parent working part-time" schedule, 71

perfectionist learners, 31–32

performing arts, 87–88

personalized learning, 129–130, 131–132

problem-based activities, 10

project-based activities, 10

proms, 85

public schools. *See* traditional schools/schooling

R

racial diversity, in homeschool community, 101–102

read-alouds, 14–15

reading list, 200

reading together, 103–104

read, learning to, 31, 59

recordkeeping, for college admissions, 153

recreation centers, 78, 86, 89

religious beliefs, 18, 102

research

on college degree of parents, 23

on college readiness and success, 159 –160

enrichment programs, 198–199

homeschool approaches, 198

sharing with naysayers, 175

roadschooling, 179

role modeling, 38

role-playing, 17

routines, 121

S

SAT exam, 155, 156

schedules, homeschool, 69–71

scholarships, college, 158–159

school districts, funding from, 79

school hours, falling behind on, 147

screen time, 15, 16–17, 62

secular curriculum, 9, 10

self-teaching, 40

sensory sensitivities, 43–44

service projects, 154–155

single parents, 178, 180

single-subject curriculum, 10, 11

socialization, 136–144

social media homeschooling groups, 80, 199

social skills, 137–138

socioeconomic status, in homeschool community, 102

spaces, homeschooling, 50–56

sports programs/events, 36–37, 85–86, 88

standardized tests, 146, 155–156, 159

standards, 110, 145–146, 150, 198

state-provided opportunities, 79

state requirements, 195

storage spaces, 55–56

strong-willed learners, 30

supplemental curriculum, 11

T

table talk questions, 18

teaching. *See also* learners; learning

definition, 58

for a learning/teaching balance, 37–39

outsourcing, 40

parent's ability for, 22–23, 25–26

teens and tweens

adapting to homeschooling, 36–37

benefits of homeschooling, 25

community for, 97

socializing with homeschool co-op, 142

testing, standardized, 109, 146, 155–156

test scores, 109

theater arts, 66, 88

theme days, 12, 65

time required for homeschooling, 60

Tim Tebow laws, 86

traditional schools/schooling

band through, 87

celebrations in, 82–83

community in, 92

comparing homeschooling with, 94

homeschoolers falling behind in school hours compared to, 147

independent study programs through, 112

learners who prefer, 35–36

participating in sports programs of, 86

transitioning to homeschooling from, 35

transcripts, 153, 158

twice-exceptional students, 163, 167, 172

U

uninterested learners, 32

unit studies, 11, 32, 84, 110, 190, 198

V

values, 17–21, 132

vestibular system, 120, 121

video instruction and lessons, 33, 40

volunteering, 115, 154

W

websites, educational, 76–77, 198

weird, stereotype of homeschooled children as, 141

Williams, Serena and Venus, 79

working families

homeschool schedule for, 71

making homeschooling work for, 181–184

statistics on, 178

Y

YMCA, 78, 86, 88, 89, 182

Acknowledgments

From Jessica

Jake, your endless love and support are the only way writing this book was possible. Thank you for inspiring me and encouraging me even when the home-cooked meals were scarce and the nights were late. Our children and I are so lucky to have you. My beautiful children, you are the reason I am passionate about homeschooling. You both show me the incredible ways learning comes naturally to you. I have been fascinated watching you learn and grow over the years and can't wait to see what lies ahead. Thank you for loving me and forgiving me for the many mistakes I make in parenting you. I love you so. Mom and Dad, thank you for taking a chance on homeschooling and trusting me to make my own educational path as a teenager. Thank you for being incredible grandparents and supporting our homeschooling journey. I love you both. Antonea, you and your friends have always been such an inspiration to me and my homeschooling plans. Thank you for loving my family so well. To Connie and Bill, the third grandparents, thank you for your love and support. To my old homeschool crew who took me into the group and showed me how amazing homeschooling could be, thank you.

From Mandi

Marcus, you make homeschooling possible for us, and I am so grateful that you love parenting our children too. Thank you. You supported this book with endless hours of time spent caring for our children and the household, reading and rereading our manuscript, and always being willing to discuss any question, argument, or research pertaining to homeschooling. Your perspective as my husband and wisdom as a dad is invaluable to me. Your love, positive attitude, and passion for homeschooling made this book possible. Micah, Ruby, and Maisy, you have shown patience, kindness, flexibility, and encouragement to me on a daily basis throughout our homeschooling journey, as well as during this new project. Thank you. I love and enjoy you, and I feel honored and blessed to get to be your mom. Mom and Dad, thank you for equipping me with a lifetime of experience, encouragement, and strength that have taught me to be unapologetically myself and to stand up for my convictions and commit to them to be the person and parent I should be. Showing me God's love my entire life filled my soul with perseverance to be who God has called me to be. Thank you to my mother-in-law, Linda, whose enthusiasm for this book and all things homeschooling have been a major encouragement for my family and me.

From Both of Us

We'd like to thank our beta readers especially, for your generous gift of time and expertise in reviewing our manuscript and for the stories you shared (with some included in this book). This book would not be the same without your experience, knowledge, and support. To our Coop Group: Your heart, inspiration, and friendship are a gift to us and our children. You have made the biggest impact of fun and joy in our current homeschool lives.

We are grateful for the contributions of the following homeschoolers whose stories are shared in this book: Jessica Ackermann, Emily Ashworth, Raszell Carpenter, Jacob Carpinelli, Sofia Carpinelli, Sarah Catania, Vanessa Clark, Valorie Delp, Johnny Durso, Leena Fana, Stephanie Fink, Debbie Garza, Charlotte Gonzales, Sharon Gully, Nikevia Lebron, Maisy McArthur, Marcus McArthur, Micah McArthur, Ruby McArthur, Jeanine Mak, Hailey Newsome, Antonea Peterson, Paxton Peterson, Alicia Sisaudia, Sarah Sleipness, Teresa Solis, Iliana Soltani, Laura Varey, Thuan Vu, Naomi Wade, and Krista Ward.

About the Authors

Jessica Carpinelli

Jessica was raised in southern California and was both traditionally schooled and homeschooled. Jessica lived the homeschooling lifestyle starting when she was in seventh grade, developing lifelong friendships. She even met her future husband in her high school homeschool group. By utilizing the options available to her, she graduated from high school at seventeen years old and entered San Francisco State University as a junior, earning her bachelor's in economics at age nineteen. Jessica brings firsthand, experiential knowledge of the homeschooling world. With her studies in child development and over twenty years of experience as a professional dance educator, she developed the children's dance program at a southern California dance studio. She coleads a medium-sized homeschool cooperative and a large social media homeschool group. She is the co-founder of The Coop Homeschool podcast and website. As an experienced homeschooling and working parent of two children, Jessica applies her understanding of child development to provide parents with confident encouragement to find an educational path best for their unique child.

Mandi McArthur, M.A. ED., MBA

Mandi grew up in southern California and thrived in the traditional school setting for her entire formal education. She became interested in child development and education while pursuing her psychology degree from UCLA. She married her college sweetheart and followed him across the country as he pursued advanced degrees. She obtained her master's degree in education and school counseling while teaching multiple subjects at a traditional junior high school and high school. After earning her MBA, she became a homeschool parent to her three children and has been homeschooling ever since. Mandi knows how to navigate the homeschool world from her life experiences as a homeschool parent, by coleading a medium-sized homeschool cooperative, attending numerous homeschool conventions, and researching homeschool strategies and ideas for her podcast and website for The Coop Homeschool. By testing various traditional and homeschooling educational philosophies, writing and utilizing a variety of curriculum, and investing in numerous communities, Mandi brings a breadth of tried-and-true practices and wisdom to potential homeschool parents.

The Coop Homeschool

Together, Jessica and Mandi started The Coop Homeschool, a homeschool consulting group for new and experienced homeschool families who homeschool by choice, with blogs, podcasts, workshops, and one-on-one consulting. This start-up began in 2020 at the beginning of the COVID-19 pandemic, serving many parents who did not necessarily choose to homeschool at first, but who have decided to leave their traditional school to pursue the less traditional route of homeschooling. The blog and podcast are available at thecoophomeschool.com.